Deep Dark and Dan
On the Bottom with the Northw

Copyrighted material
Library of Congress Cataloging-in-Publication Data
Harrison, Rebecca
Deep Dark and Dangerous: On the Bottom with the Northwest Salvage Divers
ISBN – 13: 978-1419625831
1. Salvage—Northwest 2. Pacific 3.Deep diving—Northwest Pacific

The front cover photograph is of Bob Patching getting ready to descend to work on a capsized ship.   Photograph by Larry Barber

Back cover photograph is of Rebecca Harrison peering into a Mark V helmet at the Oregon Maritime Center & Museum in Portland, Oregon.
                                        Photograph by Daniel S. Cowan

Deep Dark and Dangerous
On the Bottom with the Northwest
Salvage Divers

Rebecca Harrison

To my dearest friend, Matthew,
I hope you enjoy my book,
Rebecca Harrison

2016

In memory of Randy Greeninger, the first construction diver I met. It was his passion, dreams, encouragement, and intensity about diving that inspired this book.
                                                                            - Rebecca

CONTENTS

Fred Devine in his diving gear, 1940.
Photograph from Fred Devine & Salvage, Inc.

ACKNOWLEDGEMENTS

A great deal of the facts and information for this book were accumulated through personal interviews and correspondence. The following chapters are accounts of hardhat divers who spent their lives in the Northwest. With the help of their families, friends, and sometimes the diver himself, each chapter includes one of the diver's favorite adventures.

I would like to especially thank those divers and their families who shared their stories with me, their personal photographs, and assisted me with support in the technical aspects of construction and salvage diving. I owe much gratitude to these particular divers and companies:
(M.K.) Red Bingham, Syd and Pete Campbell with the Foss Maritime Co., Dave and Ginny Clark and the Clark Maritime Corp., Kent Cochran and Konrad Schweiger with the Advanced American Diving Service, Ken Dye, Stan Eike, Pat Joseph, Herman Kunz, Mick Leitz with the Fred Devine Diving & Salvage Co., Mike Mangold, Philip Mann, Ron McCray, J.D. Proctor, Skip Smith, Kerry Walsh.

Very special thanks are due to the family members who contributed on behalf of the divers who are no longer alive. They are:
Norma Burford, Mary Ellen Finch, Tim and Robert Finch, Jim and Paul Greenke, Herbert Lieser, Beulah Maiken, Peggy Morey, Margaret Sheats, and Fred Devine's daughters: Bonnie Pfannenstiel, Betty Riley, and Dixie Stambaugh. Also, the Fireman's Fund Insurance Company in San Francisco, California, the Historical Diving Society North American Chapter in Santa Monica, California, and the Oregon Maritime Center and Museum in Portland, Oregon.

I would also like to thank Craig Lesley, Oregon author, for guiding me with finalizing my words into an accurate and well-written book. I would like to give credit to Peter Marsh, outdoor & nautical writer and boat builder, for the use of Larry Barber's private collection of photographs and editing of my final manuscript. Also, a special thank you to my husband, Daniel S. Cowan, who proofed my manuscript, cover layout and made my photos in this book picture perfect.

Rebecca Harrison

He did a bit more than merely a "proof" on the manuscript.
—D.S.C.

Divers and tenders on Diving Barge 3505

Standing, left to right, divers: John F. Thompson, Frank P. Blair, William Thompson, Thomas J. Skailes, Klass Everts, Morris Devine, Art Zimmerman, Harry Reither, Clyde Lieser, and assistant superintendent C.J. Herbold.

Kneeling left to right, tenders: James Thompson, William Boone, Charles Stewart, Edwin Blair, Gail Jensen, Hugo Ahnger, Louis Smith, Al Lane, Virgil Risley, and L. Fowler

Photograph from the Fort Peck U:S. Army Engineering District, October 15, 1939.

WHO WERE THESE DIVERS?

The lure of the ocean, the spellbinding tales of exploration on the high seas, and the mysteries of the deep have fascinated people throughout the ages. Tall, wind-filled sails outlined against brilliant skies, dark blue swells rising and falling to the rhythm of the universe, and a fresh ocean breeze in one's face is what many of us envision. The hardworking commercial divers, those people of courage and ironclad determination whose lives are on the line each time they descend to the bottom of the sea or the murky dark of powerful rivers, do not share these visions.

Little is known about the beginnings of underwater diving. There are relics that date to 4500 BCE which have been engraved with mother-of-pearl. Various mother-of-pearl carvings have also been found in the Sixth Dynasty of ancient Thebes, around 3200 BCE. In 2500 BCE, the Chinese Emperor Yu was given beautiful figures of pearl curios.

During the growth of the Greek and Roman Empires, diving became known as a much-admired profession. There are several accounts of dive work in classical literature, such as in the *Iliad*, where Homer mentions a diver gathering seafood. Alexander the Great was said to have ordered divers to remove underwater obstacles in the harbor of a city called Tyre (Lebanon) after he had conquered it in 332 BCE. Diving for military purposes was also beginning during this same time period. Early underwater warriors were sent to cut holes in enemy ships, to build underwater defenses against enemies, and to clear harbors for the attack.

In the first century BCE, there were some commercial diving and salvage jobs in most of the major shipping harbors around the Mediterranean Sea. In some areas, laws were recognized that showed the risks of divers and provided a pay scale that increased with the salvage depth. These first commercial divers were usually given a portion of the actual items salvaged. (There are records of such a practice by the Rhodians in the reign of Perseus, 179-168 BDC.)

Unfortunately, the development of diving equipment was not seen until the early 1500s. Up until then, clasping a heavy stone to stay underwater was a common way of overcoming the sea. A smart salvager would tie a rope to the stone and leave the other end on the surface. Then, when he had run out of air or needed immediate assistance ascending, he would tug on the rope and alert his tender. His complete dive was no longer than the one or two minutes that the diver could hold his breath.

Over time, ingenuity became the best inventor. Some of the first patterns for diving helmets have been dated from the sixteenth century. These designs showed helmets made from leather with long tubes extending upward. Since air pumps and compressors weren't even imagined until the European Revolution, these hoods may have done little to help the diver while he was briefly under the surface.

In 1788, an innovation in the diving world was created when John Smeaton produced a working air pump. Now, ideas and inventions were escalating for safe diving. In 1828, two English brothers, John and Charles Deane, patented the first diving dress. (A diving dress is a heavy rubber suit, often layered inside with cotton covering the diver's body, arms, and legs. The dress is worn by entering through the neck opening that has a thick rubber gasket collar.) This invention included a helmet and a water resistant suit. The helmet had connections for simple air supply and two viewports on either side. (Unfortunately, the helmet only rested on the diver's shoulders, so water leakage was still prevalent.)

In 1819, Augustus Siebe invented the first useful deep-sea diving outfit. His diving equipment had a heavy metal helmet with three viewports, and it was attached to a breastplate. Both the helmet and the breastplate weighed 70-75 pounds each. The breastplate was joined to a short, waist length pliable jacket. This hardhat uniform worked as long as the diver was standing upright. If he bent down or turned, water could fill the jacket and drown the diver. In 1837, Mr. Siebe improved his design, which then became the ancestor of today's hardhat diving outfits.

Even now, salvage divers work underwater in blinding darkness, despite carrying hand-held lights. In their cumbersome diving gear, divers have barely enough room to move around, while at the same time fighting the cold temperatures and fast currents. It is a dirty, unromantic and highly dangerous way of earning a living. Yet, these divers would not trade their jobs for any other profession. From locating sunken boxcars to repairing concrete foundations for bridges, no task is too risky. Any underwater salvage or repair work becomes the job of these elite divers. Salvage divers must be carpenters, masons, riggers, hydraulic mechanics, ironworkers, welders, pile bucks and underwater engineers. They must be able to adapt all blueprints, tools, and supplies to the harsh realities of the underwater environment.

In the early days, divers could only work an average of two hours at moderate depths, decompressing manually at set intervals before returning to the surface. Depending on the water and weather conditions, they could work no more than three two-hour shifts in a given day. But many times, they chose to stay down longer and work later - just to get the job done.

Fallen branches, old logs and wire mesh obstructed the diver's progress and damaged his tools. Only a couple hundred feet of hose connected the diver to the safety of the barge. It was not unusual for the diver's air hose to wrap around a loose piling, sometimes even cutting the airline. If the lifeline was damaged, death hovered in the deep only minutes away.

No other profession has claimed so many lives in such an isolated place. Before the 1940s, the equipment for a diver was primitive and was put together from supplies scrounged up and concocted from his own backyard. A diving dress was not necessary for depths above thirty feet, and often a beginning diver plunged into the water outfitted with no more than a pair of tennis shoes, a bathing suit, a helmet, a hand or automobile pump and an air hose (sometimes cut from a garden hose). Because commercial helmets were very expensive, the diver's headgear was often assembled from a gasoline tin and a piece of plate glass.

A diver had to compensate for the decompression, a gradual reduction of air pressure on a person who experiences high pressure while underwater, to get the gases, such as nitrogen and helium, out of his body. Good news arrived with the invention of the "Iron Doctor," which the U.S. Navy began using in 1927. This specially designed pressurized chamber mixed helium and nitrogen into the suits, which navy divers breathed while descending as a precaution against Caissons Disease, a decompression sickness often called "the bends." Caissons Disease is caused by a rapid decrease in air pressure that causes nitrogen bubbles to form in the bloodstream. A diver could get the bends by rising to the surface too quickly. The longer a diver stayed down, the longer he would have to decompress. Whether the bubbles lodge in a joint or muscle, they can leave a man paralyzed or even kill him.

All work before the mid-1930s was performed with hand tools. Many divers kept using handsaws, cutters, and drills until much later in the decade, preferring the power of their own muscle to gas and compressed air driven tools. Compressors in the 1930s were still hand-pumped by two men on deck. Divers could take notes underwater using a piece of zinc paper and a pencil that was wrapped in string to keep the wood and the lead together. Cameras were housed in tight brass boxes with glass fronts, much like the handmade diver's helmet. These makeshift items provided little safety for the men working in the deep.

The commercial helmets of the twenties and thirties often weighed more than fifty pounds and were painful and cumbersome to wear above the surface. They were usually made of copper, with the weight distributed across the diver's shoulders. The front window was constructed of a double plate of glass. Two smaller windows were included on the sides of the helmet. All the glass was braced with copper, giving the diver a confined view, as if he were in a cage. Along the bottom of the helmet was a flange made of four flattened pieces of ten-pound lead weights that hung down over the diver's chest and back and helped the diver stay upright. The air hose was usually connected just behind the right side window and was attached from the helmet to a double-action pump, which was securely fastened to a board on deck. A long iron lever, manually pumped back and forth, gave the diver enough air to keep from suffocating. Usually, the tenders, those who manned the pumps, handled the lines and air hose and kept their eyes on the air gauge. Often, the tenders were no more than young boys eager for work.

A good diver knew how to get down four to eight fathoms (one fathom equals six feet) by swallowing air as he descended to offset the pressure. If his career was successful, he improved his apparatus by making a copper helmet with a glass set in the front, wearing lead-soled diving boots, and carrying a small hand pump to

3

regulate his air supply. When the diver made enough money to buy his own barge, he would attach the pump to the bow, securing the connection with leather washers. The hose was draped along one side of the barge, and a Jacob's ladder hung on the other. This ladder, rolled up when not in use, was often a diver's only escape from octopi, sharks, or equipment failure.

Countless salvage divers were killed on the job. Death lurked in the deep for everyone who dared to penetrate the darkness. Drowning was the number one cause of death. Some of the other reasons were: becoming entangled in their lines, impacts from loose and falling objects, and encounters with prowling creatures. The biggest fear of every diver was underwater suffocation, also known as the "the squeeze" or "burying the helmet:" caused by a quick reduction in air pressure, such as a tear in the diving dress. It resulted in a tremendous rush from the outside pressure of the water, which can become a flesh mangling, bone splintering force that can shove the diver's body into his helmet. An experienced and well-trained diver can manipulate his weight belt to offset the chances of getting the squeeze.

Early salvage divers did not learn their craft from a school or from military training. Many times these men had an older mentor who would let them tend hose, work the barge and eventually get them ready to go to the bottom. Most divers taught their children to hardhat dive, so the trade would stay in the family. As an unwritten birthright, this task usually went to the oldest son, although in Fred DeRock's case, it was passed down to his only child - his daughter Marie.

DeRock was born in Holland in 1862 and came to Oregon when he was sixteen to pursue a submarine, wrecking, and diving career. He spent twenty-two years deep-sea diving out on Oregon's northern coast in Astoria. He had been successful in building water channels in the Willamette and Columbia Rivers. DeRock was disappointed that his wife had given him a daughter, and not a son, to carry on his trade. "I'll make a diver out of her, anyway, when she gets big enough," he told his wife.[1]

Fred DeRock's business card

Marie was a shy sixteen-year-old who had just graduated from St. Patrick's School in 1912. DeRock, a determined diver and an equally determined father, set to work teaching her how to operate tools underwater in full dress. Marie prepared for her dives as her father had instructed. She put on heavy socks, flannel underwear, and slipped a fat, rounded pad over her back to take some of the weight from the helmet off her slim shoulders. She wiggled into a small rubber suit and added the rubber cuffs at the end of the sleeves. An inner collar and breastplate of metal were secured to the rubber dress. Marie's weight of 130 pounds doubled once she put on the dive gear and shoes. When the helmet was ready to be fastened, her fretting mother placed a wool cap over her curly hair first, "I don't want my daughter's hair to be mussed," she told her husband. Both parents served as anxious tenders for the adventurous girl.

The pump and the weight of the helmet were a brutal load for Marie. Supplied with a lifeline, her father and an assistant helped her to the ladder on the scow. Eagerly, she slipped into the weightless water below. Mrs. DeRock stood by the ladder with the telephone receiver strapped to her ear and the transmitter next to her mouth.

Back on board, Marie was breathless and excited about her work underwater. She found the physical and mental performances to be much more challenging than her piano practice, reading lessons, or homemaking. "At first thought," Marie told her co-workers, Pete and Jake, "it doesn't seem such a difficult thing, this going down underwater and breathing air sent from a pump by a tube. But, the physical drawbacks are great and the mental ones even more so. For every ten feet I descend, I sustain an added pressure of four-and-a-half pounds over every square inch of my body. However, the weight I wear on my shoulders and the heavy leads on my feet make considerably less inroads on my strength while I am under the water; in fact, if I don't have them on, I'd be more apt to float to the surface than stay down. But even if my weight is made less by the surrounding water, that same water clogs my efforts and resists my motion."[2]

The thrill of diving wore off quickly and Marie soon found diving more of a duty to her father than an exciting or worthwhile endeavor. She made three construction dives for her father during her school years. Once she graduated, she left home and married an engineer.

By the 1940s, the tenders that served the diver while he was underwater proved more important than an array of tools and pumps. These helpers regulated the hand pump, watched over the airlines, and timed the diver while he worked in the waters. Connected by a two-way handset, the tender also listened to the diver to make sure that his breathing was regular, and that his thoughts were clear – as divers often got confused on the bottom. The tender was the diver's lifeline. If an accident did occur underwater, it was the tender who alerted the crew of the emergency. Tenders were as good as their reputations, and divers often requested a specific man for the job. Over time, more tenders became divers as well. Lewis Smith, a former tender, later became one of Fred Devine's best divers. Smith and many other men in the Northwest lived exciting and dangerous lives undersea.

These were the underwater pioneers who constructed the foundations for bridges and helped build dams-like the Grand Coulee and the Bonneville. They were driven by the promise of high pay, high risk, and the knowledge that they alone could outsmart nature's wicked waters by salvaging, rescuing and recovering lost ships and their cargo. Against these overwhelming odds, innumerable deep-sea divers challenged the deep and risked their lives in the treacherous sea for profit, enterprise, and excitement. Their stories tell of conquest and fear in the icy waters of Northwest rivers and oceans.

*Diver Bob Patching is about to descend into the water to work
on a capsized Russian steamship beside the Port of Portland dry docks.*
Photograph by Larry Barber

7

The training ground for the salvage industry is found offshore, on and under the water, on the deck of a heaving salvage vessel, always in unusual, and most often dangerous situations. There are no classrooms anywhere in the world that can provide the experience required to qualify someone as a salvor. No review board exists that issues a certificate proclaiming a person to be a professional salvor; you either are or you aren't.

Kerry Walsh[3]

THE FINCH FAMILY: FOUR GENERATIONS OF DIVERS

Generations of the Finch family, from 1813 to the present, dived in the seas all around the world. They were the first men to dive down in the austere Alaskan waters for riches beneath the unforgiving ice pack floors. Henry Silas Finch was one of a few men who dared to dive in the Alaska territory in the 1900s. Because of his sheer willpower, he became the first diver ever to touch bottom along the Bering Sea and live to tell about it.

Henry Mason Finch and his younger brother Charles were born and raised in Scotland, and both began submarine diving for the British Navy on July 8, 1813. Henry was just sixteen years old and enjoyed the excitement of the vigorous waters. Later, when his son Mason Finch was old enough to start on his own adventures, they immigrated to America.

In 1866, Henry Mason Finch took his grandson out on his first dive off the coast of New York at the age of sixteen. Henry Silas Finch followed in his grandfather's footsteps and became a captain and master diver. He soon joined the United States Life Saving Service on the East Coast. Ten years later, he married his sweetheart, Ida. With the opportunity of a transfer to a better paying job, Finch moved his new family to Michigan City, Indiana, where he commanded the life-saving crew for the Manistee Station in Michigan. On March 23, 1886, Finch invented and patented his quick-and-easy locking rowlocks. Later, he moved to the Michigan City, Indiana Life Saving Station. From April of 1880 to the fall of 1896, Finch had spent sixteen years overseeing submarine work in over thirty harbors.

In 1896, gold fever filled Henry Silas Finch's dreams. He could taste the riches that awaited his discovery. He resigned his charge with the government and headed westward with his son, Loren Reed, to the prosperous, port town of Seattle, Washington. Ida and his other sons, Henry Jr., and Thomas, stayed behind at their home in Michigan City. By 1897, Finch had his son out for a first dive. At twenty-one years old, Loren felt the excitement his father had always talked about; he had taught him to always respect the water's power.

Loren joined his father's quest for gold and the two men traveled through the northeast territory of Washington in search of wealth. They headed to Wenatchee, on the Columbia River, then up to Oroville, near the Canadian border. The Finch's first attempts were off of a small boat they had modified to keep their dive gear, hand pumps, and tools in the smallest possible space. It should have been a lucky year for Finch since the Columbia River was high and he could load the boat directly from the Great Northern Station. Finch found no luck when his claims failed to produce and his riverboat was wrecked in the swift-flowing water.

Henry Silas Finch's Patent for his Rowlocks, March 1886.

He next went to the far north, up to the Klondike (Yukon Territory, Canada) in 1899, following the frozen Bering Strait in search of the precious ore. The men acquired a hundred horses and packed a hundred pounds of freight per horse. Battling Alaska's bitter winds and deadly ice, they lost most of their supplies and stock to the elements and arrived in Dawson with only one horse and one hundred pounds of freight left. They stayed for nearly a year but then went back to Seattle for more equipment.

While Finch was in the Klondike, he heard about the *S.S. Islander*, a 240 x 42 x 14ft. steel-hulled passenger steamer built chiefly for the Inland Passage to Skagway, Alaska. She was noted as one of the most prestigious luxury liners available. Many of the wealthy investors took her to voyage up to the Alaska territory to view their claims in the Klondike. Stories of her carrying huge bounties of rich bullion and gold dust kept breaking through Finch's life even after he returned home.

On August 14, 1901, the *Islander* was departing from Skagway, heading for Victoria, B.C. when it hit an iceberg and sank in Stephens Passage, eleven miles south of Juneau. This tragedy made the news everywhere. The steamer had gone down in 324 feet of water. She was filled to capacity and had been carrying (so the rumor went) bullion valued at over 6 million dollars, guarded by two Canadian Mounties, plus $500,000 from the passengers' personal funds. Sixty-five crewmembers and one hundred and ten passengers survived. There was much talk about the rich miners who perished on the *Islander*. Among the victims were multimillionaires, politicians, British royalty and servicemen. No one was sure of the *Islander's* whereabouts, but one thing was clear, she was too deep to be salvaged.

Within a year, Finch went to search the bottom of Stephens Passage, looking for the *S.S. Islander*. He was unable to find her and went back home disappointed. The following year, Finch went back to search for the lost ship once more. The weather turned foul and he came back to Michigan, for a second time, empty-handed.

Finch took his second son, Henry Silas Finch, Jr. on his first dive at Michigan City, Indiana in 1903. The boy was sixteen, the same age both his father and grandfather had been for their first dives. The young Henry stood cautiously at the water's edge wearing one of his father's rubber outfits and a slightly battered bronze helmet. He was afraid of the fast currents but knew his father expected courage, not fear. Young Henry was five-feet, nine inches tall, and had dark brown hair and eyes, just like his father. Poised to dive, their eyes met, his father nodded at him, and into the water young Henry went.

By 1904, Finch had heard of several men discovering gold in the Alaskan Territory. Again, he longed for those buried riches and the bullion buried in the *Islander*. Outfitted with a newly designed barge and diving bell, Finch packed his tackle on the Henry Finch tug and with his son Loren, headed off to Southeast Alaska. Some friends back in Michigan had invented the diving bell Finch took along with him. It wasn't much more than a toughened dive tank with a small port and two attached deadlights. The bell could hold only enough air for about a 30-minute submersion. This bell came with a bad history. After three earlier submersions in Michigan, the water pressure had blown out one of the deadlights and a diver drowned. This didn't stop Finch; he just made his own modifications and took it up north.

Finch succeeded in locating the *Islander*, but he could only see its shadow through the window of his bell. He saw a wide-open hole in her bow, but it was too deep for him to tackle her hold and the sunken riches. While on their way back, tragedy struck: Loren suffocated and died from undetected gas fumes on the tug. He was only twenty-eight years old.

The following winter, Finch took Henry, Jr. to Nome, Alaska, in search of gold. Their voyage was a rough journey, especially for the young boy. The first night, a huge storm roared across the gulf and mercilessly tossed the steamer about on mountainous waves. Clutching a handrail, the boy made his way down below on wobbly legs seeking safety. "This is the first diving work that will be done in this country," Finch told his son, who stood shuddering, "at least that we know of. If we make good equipment to dive with, we could get hundreds of tons; yes, thousands and maybe millions of tons." He gave the boy an encouraging smile and left him feeling safe hunkered down by the rail.

The screaming wind pierced the comfort of the cabin. The boy huddled against the rolling walls, shut his eyes and sucked in his lower lip to hide his fear from his father. The vicious storm swept away most of the vegetables, storage crates, provisions, and animal stock, including 700 chickens. Finch knew the gold was down there in the icy waters, and he was determined to find it.

Once they landed in the Alaskan territory, they traded their supplies for horses. Finch managed to cram his tools and provisions on a sled with barely enough room left for his son and himself. Packed tightly, they made it all the way north of Nome. There, he mined by using a sand-sucker hose. To accomplish this, he had to first build a portable pumping station that he placed on runners. He stored it in an old freight car, which held the engine and a centrifugal sand-sucker. He connected a line of sluices to his creation for washing the sand and separating it from the gold. To house his air pump he built a simple hut that looked like a boiler house on skis. Finch employed a few trusted men to supply him with air while he worked underwater.

Young Henry stayed loyally by his father's side in the freezing coastal winds of Alaska. Finch did all of his own diving. Cutting away at six feet of the ice with an axe, he used the best tackle available for diving. His helmet was made of bronze that had to be mounted on a frame, which was then lowered onto his head, coming to rest on his shoulder plates. His dress was made of canvas and rubber. Hand pumps generated enough air pressure for him to descend safely to between thirty and fifty feet.

Under the formless rubber dress, Finch wore a layer of thick woolen underwear. While the young boy held the diving dress, his father wriggled his way into it, inching his feet from the neck opening into the bottom of the suit. Having donned the gear, the young Finch laced up the back of his father's leggings and checked the entire dress for loose connections. When the older Finch was ready to descend, his son lifted up the heavy metal corset and placed it over his father's head so it rested its weight evenly. Butterfly nuts held the corselet screwed tightly across the diver's broad shoulders.

Trudging to the edge of the ice, Finch descended halfway into the water. His son then hoisted up over one hundred pounds of flat weight supports across his father's shoulder straps, and fastened his helmet down with brass screws. Checking it twice, Henry signaled to his father that all was secured and tight. Finch rang a bell to signal he was ready to go under.

His son began cranking the hand pump while Finch fidgeted with the air-valves in his helmet. Grabbing the guide rope, he let go of the ice edge and slipped down into the freezing blackness below. All sight was lost, and communication was limited to the rope tied to the front of Finch's dress and the hand-made submarine telephone that he had invented and patented, May 31, 1892. Using this device, he was able to maintain some connection with his son, advising him to adjust the apparatus as necessary. The young Finch had to keep a constant eye on the water and keep the ice from collecting on his father's lifeline. An accumulation of ice on these lines could cause them to crack or snap apart. There would be no chance of rescuing his father without a solid hold. Once Finch was on the bottom, he tugged on his rope, signaling to his son to start the engine of the sand-sucking machine. Guiding the suction end of the pipe manually, he could send a large load of sand up the tube on each dive.

The dutiful son, trying to ignore the biting cold, waited along the edge of the ice, ready to pass tools down the line and keeping the coffee hot for his father's ascent from the freezing water. Feeling the numbing winter wind cut sharply across his face, Henry worried about his father whose gloved hands must have felt like icicles. Gloves were bulky and burdensome but had to be used to keep his hands from freezing underwater.

Trying to focus on the job, Finch refused to let the icy water play with his wits. He'd known too many men who ended up with the bends because they let their minds wander from their task. The cold was not only physically tough on his body, but it could make him lose his train of thought and become confused or forgetful.

The closer Finch got to the shoreline, the more he had to crawl. The thick sheets of ice that threatened to keep him pinned down hindered his progress; nevertheless, he continued his pursuit for gold. Driven by his passion, he searched every inch of the waters. He crept on his belly in order to get as close to shore as possible with his suction machine, hoping to find a score of immeasurable wealth hiding on the bottom. Due to the isolation, he dug, without the usual worry of someone jumping his claim!

Completing the day's work, Finch would begin his ascent, stopping intermittently to decompress. First, wrapping his feet through the guide rope for balance, he came up to forty feet below the surface for a rest. He rose ten more feet and waited for twenty minutes. At ten more feet, he held again for twenty-five minutes. At this level, he was fully decompressed and gave a tug on the rope signaling that he was ready to surface. Finch felt chilled to the bone for hours after the dive. Hugging the stove, he told young Henry, "I am going to chatter the enamel off my teeth."

Some days he brought up as much as $90 worth of gold from the ocean bottom. Not every day was that profitable. There were many days when both men stayed huddled inside the shack because the piercing winds blew too hard, or the diving equipment was frozen solid like steel, or the steam line iced over and frost made icicles on the boiler. When they found enough bullion to do business, the men went into Nome for trade, where they heard many rumors of hidden ships filled with treasures.

Finch searched up north for another year. After exhausting all possible stretches along Nome, he finally took his son back to Seattle. He then returned to Michigan and moved his entire family to the Pacific Northwest. He continued to dream about the *Islander* while rescuing several wrecks along the Columbia and in lower Alaska. In 1905, he created the diving and wrecking company of Henry Finch & Son, comprised of Capt. Finch, Sr., and his son, Captain Henry Finch, Jr. When not working for their salvage company, the men went treasure hunting.

In the spring of 1906, Finch went north to St. Michaels, Alaska, to recover lost cargo from the sunken *SS Valencia*. Later, in the fall of that same year, after forty-two days on the Columbia River, he raised the craft, the *W.H. Pringle* from the Entiat Rapids. Finch won fame for these great feats. In 1907, he recovered the *Minnie E. Kelton*, the first wreck raised and removed from the Columbia River Bar. The danger was always present during the diving expedition, and death teased the divers at every depth. Once, when Finch was down sixty feet off the Colman dock in Washington, the air valve in his helmet froze. He could not get any more air and had only the oxygen remaining in his diving dress. He quickly declared his emergency by giving three tugs to his lifeline and was brought to the surface. Being near death did not stop him. Though feeling faint, he fixed his air valve and returned to the job below.

Finch had become renowned all over the northwest, not only for breaking the dive record by staying under thirty-eight feet for over five hours, but also for his success at finding gold. His ingenious method of salving the steamer *Kitsap* in Seattle brought his name to the attention to the newspapers all over the West Coast. This operation was considered the finest piece of salvage work ever completed in the world.

The *Kitsap* had been struck by a steamship, the *Indianapolis*, and sank in a thick blanket of fog on December 14, 1910. In less than twenty minutes, she went down in 240 feet of water, about 800 feet into the bay from Pier Four. "I have been in the service of the company 37 years," said Superintendent Engineer Nelson of the Elliot Bay Dry Dock Company. "I have been involved in marine matters and investigated many wrecks, but I have never in all this time known of a vessel sinking so quickly as the *Kitsap* dropped beneath the waters on Elliot Bay."

The excessive depth made the men's salvaging efforts nearly impossible. It was a wild gamble, funded by the Elliot Bay Dry Dock Company, but the Finch divers successfully met the challenge. Finch sent a message to his son in Tacoma asking him to help with the job. "Am sending the balance of crew south on the Northwestern 19th. Return to the wreck tomorrow and then return to Seattle. As she lies in deep water, looks like the ship might be a total loss, but we might get the mail and purser's safe by trudging at low tide. Investigation before inspector's completed."

Unable to send a diver 240 feet below meant that the crew had to position a dry dock over where the steamer had gone down, and a long cable had to be anchored at the bottom of the bay, ten feet away from the wreck. Using a small tug, the men took the other end of the cable and circled around the bay slowly, searching the bottom. After only a few hours of sweeping, the hull was located. Marked with buoys, several lines were dropped around the steamer, outlining her shape.

The men hooked under each end of the *Kitsap*, behind her propeller and forward of midship. These two cables were then connected to each other near the center of the steamer. Since the location of the wreck was too deep for diving, slipping an iron loop over the attached cable lines did the work. Three days later, when the men were ready to lift the steamer, the grappling lines snapped under the ship's weight. The dry dock the men were using had the capacity to lift 600 tons, but the cables snapped under the ship's 100 tons. Time went by while more cables were attached. Finally, the men were able to drag the *Kitsap* within a half-mile from shore, near Pier 11. At the same time, divers hooked onto anything they came in contact with and managed to raise the number 4 lifeboat from the top of the *Kitsap*'s bow. Bags of mill feed and various cargos also broke free from the wreck below.

All went smoothly until the steamship, *H.B. Kennedy*, passed by and somehow came too close to the marked buoys where the men were working. The swell caused by her passing flooded the diving barge and nearly knocked the divers into the sea.

Recovered from the troublesome incident, the men continued their work late into the night; nothing would stop them from completing their salvage. Even at that extreme depth, Finch's son Henry was able to go down and make his way through the blackness to hook seven cables under the *Kitsap*'s massive hull. Once these cables were secure, the successful outcome of the salvage work was almost certain. Henry came up on board joyous that his father was pleased by a job well done.

With the *Kitsap* fastened down, the men pulled her to West Seattle, where she was examined and salvaged. The next day, her hull was pumped and patched until she could float independently. Now the *Kitsap* was ready to be pulled by Finch's scow, the *Yellow Jacket*, to the Elliot Bay dry dock on the East Waterway for overhaul and repair. In spite of this, to the shore men watching the battered and bruised *Kitsap* in tow, she appeared beyond repair. With her broken timbers and upper works, shattered house, mud-bespattered hull and her inability to proceed under her own steam, doubt reflected in the men's eyes. Their misgivings did not stop Finch from bringing the *Kitsap* into the dock with her twenty-seven flags flying proudly in the wind. When all the damage was repaired, she was seaworthy and became the first successful salvage job ever completed anywhere in the United States at the depth where she sank.

Finch trained his youngest son, twenty-one-year-old Thomas Reid Finch to dive in 1911. The Finch men were dedicated salvagers and true enterprisers. One of their first major successful salvages came from a wooden hull steamship, the *Ramona*. The Pacific Coast Steamship Company in the Seattle-Southeastern Alaska route operated the *Ramona*. She was a joint passenger/freight carrier. During a southbound trip in September of 1911, she struck the rocks off North Spanish Island in the Alaskan Territory. The *Ramona* went down in ten fathoms of water. The hull was badly beaten by the rocks that twisted the freighter and cracked her in two; the masts were bent ten to twelve feet.

Fortunately, the passengers were saved and were transferred to the steamship, *Northwestern*, en route to Seattle. The remaining crewmembers of the *Ramona* camped on the shore of Spanish Island in tents, made from the canvas given to them by the crew of the steamship *Delhi*. They lived off the ship's emergency provisions and the canned salmon carried in by the tide. The cargo, which included 12,000 cases of salmon and over $150,000 in gold in her hold, was lost.

Hired by Captain E.L. McNoble, the Finch family went in search of the lost ship near the spot where the *Ramona* supposedly sank. They took the steamship Humboldt, up to Wrangell, Alaska. The men sailed on a tug with an additional barge for their salvage work on North Spanish Island. Fighting the familiar freezing weather, the older Finch set up the barge over the location where the *Ramona* was last seen. His son Henry was first to go down searching for the lost ship. Although the senior Finch was certain of his son's skills of the trade, he watched Henry's preparation with a critical eye. (Finch, now a rugged man of 61 years, went down to salvage the wreck of the *Ramona* at least four times.)

Henry removed his work clothes and put on heavy woolen raiment under his canvas-rubber diving dress. The father adjusted the ropes for his son's descent. After climbing into his bulky shield of rubber and diving dress, Henry sat down. Thomas yanked the diving dress up and slowly worked it over his brother's feet and legs. The upper part of the dress was then pulled up, and Henry pushed his fingers, hands, and arms into the sleeves. Henry's hands were left bare, his wrists gripped tightly by the rubber band that prevented water from entering the outfit. Finch then assisted Thomas in lifting the metal corselet over Henry's head and placing it onto his shoulders. Next, Henry put on his heavy, brass-weighted boots. Finally ready to dive, he signaled and went over to the ladder that was attached outside the barge. When he was halfway into the water, Thomas placed flat weights over his shoulders on straps, positioned the helmet with its air pipe and valves over Henry's head and screwed it onto the metal corselet.

Now that Henry was geared, he adjusted the air supply by working the valves in his helmet. He climbed down the ladder, which extended over six feet below the barge, and guided himself down to the bottom with a "shot rope," a rope with a weight on the end. The only communication between Finch and his son Henry was a phone line and a rope fastened on the diver's chest. Maneuvering along the bottom of the ocean, Henry searched his surroundings and quickly located the demolished hulk of the *Ramona* looming in the distance. As he approached the wrecked hull, he noticed how hollow and lifeless this once magnificent liner was, as it lay surrounded by busy sea life.

Having sited the *Ramona,* Henry ascended to the barge. He adjusted his air supply valve to give himself buoyancy. As he floated upwards, he let his hands glide up the rope, stopping at certain depths, wrapping his legs around the rope to hold himself steady. He made his way up slowly, stopping at certain intervals to allow for decompression. At ten feet below the surface, he stayed in place for about fifteen minutes, decompressed enough to safely return to the barge.

Every time Henry came up, he nearly froze from the icy grip the waters had on him. When the bulky gloves came off, his fingers looked like purple sausages. On his last dive, Henry located the safe, which had gone through a hole in the side of the hull. It took several dives each for Henry, Thomas and their father to recover gold bars and dust worth $16,000. In addition, the men were able to rescue several letters and packages they found floating like seaweed about half a mile from the wreck. The *Ramona*'s remaining riches, papers, and several hundred dollars were lost forever.

The men were also successful in recovering some of the lost bullion, valued at $112,000. While the men pulled the bullion safely to shore, memories of their exploring days in Alaska came flooding back. The only difference was that the water temperature here was far above the freezing temperatures of the Arctic. Rumors raced along the dock about previous divers who struck it rich and were murdered for their treasures. Fearing sabotage and thieves, the Finch men took turns guarding their treasure. For the ten days of travel before cashing in their salvaged golden haul in Wrangell, they sacrificed sleep protecting their bounty against pirates. Finch knew how to catch a few winks while resting his arm on a loaded rifle. Henry soon learned this trick from his father. The senior Finch sailed back stateside, taking his sons back to Seattle.

The Finch family had salvage operations active all along the waters from Washington to Alaska. In February of 1920, tragedy struck them yet again, when Thomas caught pneumonia while rescuing a drowning father and a seven-year-old boy from Lake Whatcom in Washington. This heroic deed cost Tom his life, as he was exposed too long to the cold waters of the lake; he died from pneumonia at age twenty-nine.

Even after Thomas's tragic death, the men didn't stop diving. One of their most noteworthy accomplishments was the raising of 253 drums of creosote that had gone down in sixty feet of water at Eagle Harbor, Washington. The drums were being loaded on the scow, *Sardhana*, when winds made the crew lose control, and the cargo rolled off into the water. In less than four days time, the men had recovered the drums at a rate of twenty an hour.

At that time, the *A.J. Fuller*, a wooden square-rigger, built in 1881, traveled the west coast. She worked at the end of Puget Sound-Australian timber trade and made a lot of money for her owners. The ship was also engaged in the Alaskan salmon sea trade, carrying cargo between Uyak, Kodiak Island and Seattle. On October 30th, 1918, dense fog blanketed Elliot Bay. The *Fuller* was loaded with canned fish and other cargo. At one o'clock in the morning, an O.S.K. trans-Pacific steamship, the *Mexico-Maru*, entered the port and collided with the wooden three-master. The *Fuller* received a ten-foot tear in the starboard bow. Because of her heavy load, she sank within ten minutes in two hundred and twenty-five feet of water. 48,000 cases of canned salmon and 4,000 barrels of salt fish were swallowed by the bay.

"I'll go down to the tops and stays in her mast," Henry announced. He then asked his father to tend him. Henry descended to the upper yards of the submerged ship that lay seventy feet below the surface. Using grappling hooks, he brought up the ship's compass and other fittings. All salvage operations came to a halt when the insurance company laid claim to the *A.J. Fuller's* cargo that the company had claimed as lost. The insurance underwriters did not believe the sunken ship in Elliot Bay was the *Fuller*. Both Finch and Henry proved them wrong. Henry dived more than 200 feet down to recover a piece of her nameplate and presented it as evidence to the insurance company. He was then asked if the *Fuller* was a menace to other vessels anchoring in the harbor. This question was frequently asked of knowledgeable old timers on the harbor, and in this case, Henry reassured them that this square-rigger was not a menace.

"Merchant vessels never drop their 'hooks' in such deep water," he explained. "Teredo worms and the chemical action of the salt water are solving the risk problem. The masts of the *Fuller* are down by this time and there probably is very little of the vessel left, except the hull. She had a full cargo which I'll bet has been destroyed." After listening to the report, the insurance agents directed Henry to go down again. They hoped to salvage all of her cargo.

"There is a pressure of one-half pound to the foot of depth or a total of 112 ½ pounds where the *Fuller* is lying, and combined with the chemical action of the water, long ago destroyed the cargo."[4] Henry tried to inform the men. "The ship could have been raised by using sweep wires and barges, but you underwriters decided the salvage operations would be too expensive." He pointed accusingly at both of the men.

"You didn't want to spend the money on the value of the vessel and the water-soaked cargo", he said as he stormed past the men. To this day, because of the insurance dispute, the *A.J. Fuller* still lies untouched in the Seattle Harbor, 2,000 feet offshore and 240 feet down.

One of their more successful projects was a job with the city of Seattle. City engineers were indebted to Finch and his son for taking on the laying of deep-water outfall pipe from the Denny Way, and a water main across the West Waterway to Seattle, and a large sewer main near West Point Light. Three other companies had tried, but could not get deep enough to lay the pipe. The engineers were ready to abandon the project when the Finch divers stepped in for its completion.

This essential runway into deep waters for the northern waterfront of Seattle was being polluted by sewage emptying along by the shore. This pollution and its smell, running for three-quarters of a mile, had made it impossible to build stores or businesses. Finch, Henry, and a woman diver laid a cement cradle for the forty-four pipes that weighed 9,000 pounds apiece.

Aileen "Alys" McKey Bryant, a diver and pilot in her early twenties, was hired by Finch to go down in the West Waterway and attach a heavy chain to one of the huge pieces of pipe the men had removed from the waterway to make way for the new supply pipes. The Henry knew of Bryant because of her reputation as a superb aviatrix and a daring diver. She became the first woman pilot to make a solo flight in Canada. Bryant made her famous flight at the Minoru Racetrack in Richmond on July 31, 1913. It was the first day of a three-day show by the "iron-nerved aviatrice Alys McKey" and her husband, "death-defying aviator Johnny Bryant." (The couple had married two months before, but that wasn't widely known and press still referred to McKey by her maiden name.) Finch initially found her to be a novelty, the only female submarine diver he had ever heard of or met. He hired her for small jobs and was immediately impressed with her proficiency and dive work. Often, when Bryant was available, Finch employed her as a back-up diver.

The divers were now ready to lay the sewer pipe. Each pipe was twelve feet long and forty-eight inches wide and totaled 532 feet in length. The depth of the water ran as much as fifty feet at high tide, which made the divers' job extremely dangerous. Assisted by Wallace Blain, John Bane, and other divers, the crew completed the task in record time.

While laying pipe in the deep end of the Denny trunk sewer, the tenders on the Finch barge were surprised to see Henry shoot up out of the water, his diving ensemble inflated like a big rubber balloon. Reeling him in by his lifeline, they finally hauled the "balloon" onto the barge. As they unscrewed his helmet, the air came rushing out. Wanting to see what the commotion was, Finch who was also on board, rushed to his son's side. The shaken young Henry told how a shark had bitten off one of his lead-soled boots, which threw him off balance and forced him to come up from the bottom, feet first. The air became trapped in his dress instead of being expelled from the check valve, creating his balloon-like appearance. The men laughed at the young diver's story, as they knew there were no dangerous sharks anywhere near Puget Sound. A few minutes later, John Bane, came up. He had been running a dredging hose, using it to make a trench in the bottom mud for the sewer pipe. He was upset that his line was plugged and thought he sucked up a fish. The men laughed when they found Henry's boot bent in half by the pressure of the hose.

Captain Henry Finch, Sr., known as the "King of Divers," was a very successful 75-year-old millionaire when he died in 1926. Three years later, Henry heard more stories about the *S.S. Islander* and its sunken value. As rumors circulated, the number of drowned victims increased along with the wealth purportedly in their possession. Even though Henry had dived in waters from the freezing temperatures of the Bering Sea to the tropical waters of southern California; Henry's mind was still occupied with speculation about the *Islander*. He wouldn't let it rest, and hired by the Curtis-Wiley Expedition, he took his father's charts and sailed off on the *S.H. Finch* tug. Henry offered to go down in an iron diving cage, created by one of the backers, Carl Wiley. It was about forty-eight inches wide, with handles inside which operated exterior claws on the cage.

On his first descent, the tide grabbed hold of the cables and swung his tank like a giant pendulum from a grandfather clock. He could not see anything on the bottom of the sea, and only by attaching additional cables and a row of searchlights was Henry able to descend into the uncharted depth and locate the *Islander*. He concluded that she had gone down by her bow and that the collected air inside had destroyed much of her after-deck. Henry came upon several skeletons in her holds. He was unable to leave the safety of the tank to proceed with salvage activities. Both Henry and Captain Thomas Quinn went down several times to try to salvage the *Islander*. (Years later, in 1934, the *Islander* was finally hauled onto the beach, and since Finch, Sr. wasn't alive, he never got to see the ship that cost him a son and occupied years of his life. The total gold recovered was only about $50,000, which was found in the purser's safe.)

When it came time to acquaint Robert Finch, the grandson of Henry Finch, Jr., with the waters, he, like his father, was just sixteen-years-old. Although Robert eventually became a Navy Seabee and went diving with his father, he did not choose deep-sea diving as a career. He chose a path unrelated to diving: he became a salesman instead.

FRED DEVINE: PIONEER SALVAGE MASTER

Fred Devine, a noted Northwest salvage master, and diver, accomplished more than 300 salvage operations during his lifetime. Much of his success was due to his ingenuity and his impressive craft, the Salvage Chief, which Fred created and designed from a World War II surplus LSM hull in 1949.

Born in 1898, in Ord, Nebraska, George Fredrick Thomas Devine was the second of four sons. He moved with his family to Washington State when he was still a scrappy young boy. For Fred Devine and his boyhood companions, the Columbia River was the backdrop for pirating, swimming, exploring and making money. Spending his childhood on Lieser Point in Image, Washington, a defunct, runty railway stop three miles west of Vancouver, Devine mastered the water at an early age. Within a few years of their move, his father died. All of Devine's brothers went to work farming and hauling supplies for local businesses, to help support their mother. Devine headed straight for the water. In 1909, the water near his hometown offered him a way to make a profitable living.

At the age of eleven, Devine became a gillnet snag diver for some of the old fishermen along the wharves of the Columbia River. Snag diving is going down to the bottom of a river where fishing nets have been dropped. When branches or rocks catch in the gillnet, a diver is sent down to follow the snag and remove the obstructions. It is critical that the diver is strong and quick. He must follow the line that leads to the snag, kicking and pulling himself along in the water's fast currents. He must then attach a cable to the obstruction holding the net down. While grappling at the snag to keep it open to catch the fish with one hand, he then must hold onto the net with his other hand in order to keep from being swept downstream. If the snag comes loose in his grasp, the whole net could sweep him off balance with the power of a Mack truck. If he gets tangled in the net, he must cut his way out with a knife. Once the snag has been successfully cabled, the diver tugs on the cable rope twice, and he is hauled by a winch onto the snag barge. Devine filled the need for someone tough and dauntless to dive down deep, and with the ability to hold his breath for a long time underwater, he made good money clearing nets.

His mother refused to take all of his hard-earned money, so Devine invested some of his earnings into his own gear. The young diver had dreams of owning a fishing company, and with his wages, he bought his own fishing weights and nets. Word spread fast about this husky, red-haired, Irish boy who would dive great depths in the Columbia. He tried to stay in school to learn more reading and writing, but Devine soon found it too difficult to work and attend school at the same time and decided that one of them had to go. He never saw a classroom again, having only completed the eighth grade.

Fred Devine
Photograph by Larry Barber

When Devine wasn't busy with his diving work, he enjoyed achieving new goals with his swimming skills. His strong build was giving him powerful muscles. Daring the swift flow of the river, Devine made a bet to swim across the mile-wide Columbia River to the Oregon shore. His friend Earl rowed alongside, keeping an eye on him and cheering him on to victory.

Shortly after his fifteenth birthday, while Devine was diving for missing tools along the pier, his neighbor, Clyde Lieser, spotted him. When the young man came to shore, Lieser was waiting for him. "I've got a bridge repair job," Lieser said looking the young Devine over. "I need another diver. How about working for me?" Devine knew the Lieser family was well known in the Vancouver area. Except for Clyde, the Lieser men had become doctors and the women were teachers. Lieser had followed his own path and became a well-established diver and fisherman. Now in his later years, Lieser had built his own gillnet fishing boat. He wanted Devine to haul and layout fishing nets along the bottom of this powerful river. Since Devine did not fear the sweeping cold river and he needed steady work, he eagerly accepted Lieser's offer.

Devine learned all about the diving technology that was available to divers in the mid-1920's. Lieser taught him how to hold his breath underwater. The two men made a great team, and Lieser soon taught Devine all about making a living off of the resources along the Columbia. Lieser was a patient diving teacher, and Devine the ever-eager student. While wearing only his underwear, Devine swam down into the cold waters searching for salvaged goods. (Skin diving was not yet a popular method of diving.) He also practiced the mysterious art of block and tackle, locating hidden vessels, and surveying for damage on grounded freighters. Devine also learned what to do in case of an emergency and how to stay calm when something fouled the airline.

Under the guidance of his teacher, Devine acquired the skills he needed to become more than just a competent snag diver. The men were busy day in and day out with building and repairing bridge piers, as well as working for the shipyards. One of Devine's first big construction jobs with Lieser was building the new interstate highway bridge between Oregon and Washington. Under his teacher's masterful guidance, Devine evolved from a novice diver into a highly accomplished professional. (Clyde Lieser later became a diving inspector for the city of Portland, Oregon. He and Devine remained good friends until Lieser's death in the 1960s.)

Diving paid well, and while approaching his sixteenth birthday, Devine had saved enough money to purchase a diving establishment, the Sterling Diving Service, from a retired diver, Walter Sterling. (He later renamed the company Fred Devine Diving Company.) With both Lieser and Sterling's guidance, Devine expanded the small business and hired a few old pals and molded them into professional salvagers who could help him with the work.

The divers began to practice the real life of a salvager, raising small hulls and barges, dredging the river for lost tugs, and keeping enough snag diving jobs on the side to pay their bills. The jobs steadily rolled in and Devine's reputation grew.

After the war, on July 1, 1918, Devine Diving Co. was hired to locate and salvage a Portland Railway, Light & Power Company train that had gone off track into the Clackamas River, near the River Mill power plant in Estacada, Oregon. The bridge across the river had buckled under the huge weight of the freight train that had attempted to cross earlier that Thursday morning. The bridge was reduced to splintered bits of wood and broken tresses, dropping the engine into the water below.

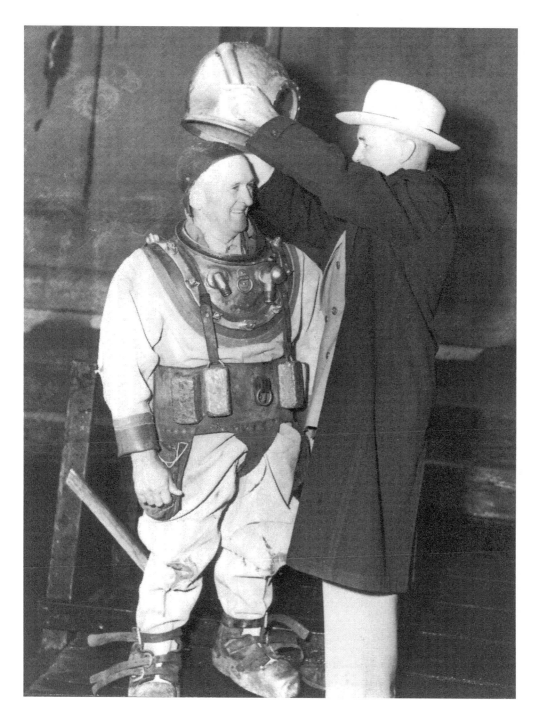

Clyde Lieser prepares to go underwater
Photograph from the Oregon Historical Society (#CN 012257)

Harold Kleineline, the trolley man, went down with the train. By sheer luck, Kleineline was sheltered from the fallen engine by the demolished bridge timbers in a small space of water. After fighting his way to the surface, he heard the cries of the injured brakeman, Ralph Kearney. He went back down into the wreckage and climbed over the debris to the damaged boxcar where Kearney was holding on, fighting for his life.

"I was tempted to jump when I first heard the bridge crack but refrained from taking the chance when I saw the timbers falling all about me," Kleineline explained to Devine. "The motorman was at his post beside me, but I do not believe he left the cab. I jumped out and fortunately escaped."[5] Along with train components, the lifeless bodies of the conductor, A. G. Kinder, and the motorman, William Murray, were lodged under the timber below the surface of the Clackamas River. The body of Kinder was later found, but not Murray's.

Devine was hired to locate Murray's body and to salvage the train engine and cars. Along with his assistant, Irvine Matoon, the two men packed more than one hundred feet of hose for their dive. After much anxious searching, the body was located downstream. Following the recovery of Murray's body, the men returned to the river and located the two electric locomotive engines and the two boxcars still lodged under the timber below the surface of the Clackamas River. This heroic feat made the headlines of the Oregon Daily Journal on July 12, of 1918. Devine was praised for successfully salvaging the train that had come to rest along the Clackamas River near the River-Mill power-plant station in Estacada.

His business boomed as job after job poured in. When World War I came along, Devine joined other divers building waterways and pier supports for the Grant-Smith-Porter and Standifer shipyards in Vancouver, Washington. When the interstate highway bridge was built across the Columbia River, Devine worked setting the huge foundation piers. After the war was over, he and his men renewed their salvage and diving efforts in the Oregon waters. Devine, still in his early twenties, was learning new skills and perfecting the trade of a salvager.

When he was twenty-five, Devine met Art Zimmerman, a seasoned diver and salvage master. The two men merged their companies and became equal owners in the Devine and Zimmerman Diving Company. (This company was the forerunner of today's Fred Devine Diving & Salvage Incorporation, located in Portland, Oregon.) These two dauntless divers tackled some of the toughest jobs in the Northwest - from sunken tugs off Cape Disappointment, Washington, to many complicated, exacting survey works. Devine and Zimmerman pursued risky salvage jobs in order to keep their business afloat. The higher the risk, the higher the rates for the salvaging job. They rarely said "No," to a dive job.

Many of the wrecks the men took on were floated in adverse conditions and called for great financial and physical risk. They often had to work in fast currents and were obliged to dive no more than two hours each day. One freighter, in particular, a steamer called the *Sea Thrush*, became stranded one foggy night in 1932. The 8,800-ton freighter ran aground on the Clatsop Spit just inside the mouth of the Columbia River, rupturing her seams and surrendering to the river. Devine and his two assistants sailed a tug through the fog, boarded the sinking steamer and secured her hatches in order to protect the cargo while the river strained and pulled at her.

With more tugs, the crew towed her through 2,000 feet of shoal water, trying to head towards deeper soundings. Heavy swells rose against her and Devine could hear the seams crack under impact; she began to snap open. Quickly, the men cut their towlines and ran their tugs away from the shattered vessel. Looking back at the sea, Devine sadly watched as the *Sea Thrush* was scattered by the violent waves that crashed against her hull. She came apart; her wreckage was strewn along the shore; bits and pieces floated in with the tide. There was nothing left to salvage and he never forgot about losing the *Sea Thrush*.

Shortly after that incident, on March 23rd, 1933, the *S.S. President Madison*, a transpacific passenger ship, owned by American Mail Line, working out of Seattle to the Orient, was lying at the repair dock of the Todd dry-dock in Seattle. It had four shell plates removed from the ship's side, opening up a hole 90 by 6 feet, only four feet above the water's edge. The haul of a scow loading timber alongside her created a huge rush of water that rolled the *Madison*. It was enough of a surge to allow an inflow of water into to her holds that broke the ship's moorings. With the bulk of the ship listing over, it drowned one man in the engine room and confined others inside the hull. The shipyard workers fled for safety, and the Coast Guard rescued the trapped individuals through the portholes. The *Madison* rammed into the sternwheeler *Harvester*, sinking her, before going on to damage the freighter *North Haven* and several smaller vessels.

Fred Devine was called to rescue the *Madison*, which was punctured in several places. "Well, I'll be hog tied," Devine remarked when he heard about the conditions required to rescue the *Madison*. Devine called on Art Zimmerman to help him refloat this fine fleet ship. He sent divers down day and night while the men rigged beach gear and set up numerous pumps on the decks of the wreck. Devine worked both from the vessel and from the shore. While divers were underwater closing off leaks long enough to pump out several compartments, the men on shore were busy rigging long jacks, which reached from the shore to the bow. These would be used to move the wreck into deeper water.

Both Devine and Zimmerman advised the divers about which leaks to patch and which ones could wait until she was safely in harbor. Devine had the whole operation in hand and the *Madison* was soon ready for the big drag. With the blow of a whistle, thousands of gallons of water started to pour from the holds of the ship. The men on the jacks tightened their slack and the workers on shore started their winches. They kept pulling with the giant tackles hauling in the cables until they were stretched to their maximum. Success rang in the sounds and whistle of machinery as the

Madison groaned and moved with the cables. The pumps had to keep going, and more leaks appeared requiring repair, and some of the patches needed more concrete reinforcement. Once at sea, divers were busy checking her from stern to bow, including the in-takes, propeller, and rudder. With her pumps still in place, the *Madison* soon set off for home under her own power.

[After six years of idleness, Jose Cojuangco, a Manila sugar magnate sold *President Madison* to Philippine interests. It was said that $35,000 in cash was brought to Seattle in a suitcase in exchange for the liner. Skippered by Captain C.J. Onrubia, the vessel was given minor repairs and a new name, *President Quezon*. She sailed for the Orient, via Long Beach, California with a 10,500-ton cargo, but while going to the assistance of a vessel in trouble, she herself ran hard aground off the island of Tanegashima, Japan on January 16, 1940, and became a total loss.]

Even his success in saving this ship didn't satisfy Devine. He knew there was a better way to reach damaged vessels in the open seas. Spending many nights hunched over his desk, he designed what he thought could be the perfect salvage craft. Not having any money to pursue his ideas at the time, he tucked his designs into a drawer in his desk.

Later in 1933, he married his childhood sweetheart, Lena Wagoner and they settled into their home on Swan Island, Oregon. His wife played an active role in the business and supported Devine in the pursuit of his dreams. "She knows exactly what I'm trying to do," Devine claimed smugly to his brother, Morris. "When I'm out of touch, she gives the orders. She's wonderful. I couldn't get along without her." Devine relied not only on Lena but on his entire family. He hired his two brothers, Morris and Chuck, and they became a part of his independent small company named Devine Diving Service. There was plenty of work available along the Columbia and the young businessman began to expand his company's activities to other rivers and inlets along the Pacific shoreline.

In 1937, the Italian motor ship, the *Feltre*, sank when it collided with the *Edward Luckenbach*, an American steamship. The collision took place in the Columbia River near the site of the former, Trojan Nuclear Power Plant. Devine and Zimmerman were hired by the Corps of Army Engineers to float the *Feltre* from the river channel. This was a difficult job, as the men had to patch a 250-foot long hole that was more than 25 high. Devine met this impossible task with great ingenuity by constructing huge timber and canvas patches which divers then secured to the damaged side of the ship. The men then pumped out enough water from the hull to raise the motor ship just enough for towing to a Portland dry-dock.

According to maritime law, compensation is paid by the owners of the ship for the services performed by the salvors. This includes saving the vessel or goods from the perils of the sea, from wreckage, fire or other disasters. Owners and salvors agree on the amount of the money to be paid. The owners of the stranded vessels usually pay the divers their full rate regardless of the turnout. If a disagreement does occur, the amount is then fixed by the United States District Court, unless both parties agree ahead of time to accept the services of an arbitrator. The outcome of arbitration then became legally binding. Sometimes Devine would bid an "all-or-nothing job" in which case he would take any loss. This is referred in the salvage business under Lloyd's Standard Form of Salvage Agreement as "No Cure - No Pay."

Some salvage jobs took months to complete, consuming the efforts of the whole company. Many times the men found themselves out in the open sea, where thick fog or rain kept them miserably cold day after day. The Pacific Northwest weather toyed with Devine, sometimes paralyzing his work for days. Vessels that had wrecked thousands of miles from the Columbia, took his crew days to reach. Unpredictable weather proved a worthy opponent for Devine and his team of salvors.

Once a wreck was ready to be moved, with its leaks patched and the water pumped out, it still took time to get it inshore. For example, a wreck with thirty feet of water holding down her deck could take more than six days to get to the harbor. Soft mud or sand along the route delayed the process further. That was the case when Devine was bringing in the *Eagle Courier*; he had to tow her nonstop to prevent her from sinking. If a ship dropped her bow too low and sank into the sand, more patching would be required. (Patches in the water are made of concrete, boards or even canvas - anything that will stop the leaks. It is a continual process all the way to the docks.) Pumps had to be manned at all hours to keep the water from filling her hull, or flushing through her hatches, so she would stay afloat.

Devine was familiar with every part of the Columbia River - its eddies, sandbars and trick tides. His company made enough money to keep the business going, but not enough to replace much of their tattered supplies. He was quick to modify, repair and adapt their equipment for each particular job. While he expected his men to follow his example, Devine never sent a diver down for a job that he would not have done himself.

When taking on dangerous jobs, Devine found himself staring death in the face more than once. On one occasion a loose snag smashed into his faceplate, shattering the glass. He quickly tugged on his lifeline signaling his tender to bring him to the surface before he ran out of any air to breathe. Beating death at its own game turned Devine into a veteran diver at a very young age.

The late mid-thirties saw one of Devine's most noteworthy achievements. He was signed with the Corp of Engineers on the great Bonneville Dam project on the Columbia River. For two and a half years, Devine supplied all the underwater divers and services during the building of this dam. He used his brother Morris and a noted West Coast diver, Harry Reither, to manage the underwater work. This project so impressed Devine, that he and Lena named the first of their four daughters, Bonnie.

With his baby in his arms, Devine promised that he would be there to guide her throughout her life. He never forgot how lonely it was for him when he lost his own father. He was protective of all of his daughters during their growing years and rarely did he ever let them get involved with his diving activities. "It's a man's job," he would tell the girls when they wanted to help their father.

The completion of his work on the Bonneville Dam gave Devine the opportunity to put much of what he had learned into practice. But experience turned out to be a cruel teacher. During one of his dives when he was shutting off the bays, the river rushed through the traps with unexpected velocity. Devine clutched at the bay, hanging on for his life as the river threatened to push him through the concrete traps. His air hose became slack and wrapped itself around a steel-reinforcing rod. At the same moment, his air valve froze. Having left his knife on the barge, he had no way of cutting his air hose and freeing himself from the deathtrap that had him slammed against the side of the dam.

Crawling on his stomach, he inched his way through the bitter-cold water over to his entangled air hose. Each tiny movement left him exhausted. Finally, he was able to release his air hose from the steel pipe-and promptly passed out. The tenders above knew something was wrong when they felt the tension leave his hose, and they quickly pulled him up to the surface. Devine was unconscious and his men carried him to a waiting emergency vehicle equipped with a compression chamber. Devine was lucky to avoid decompression sickness after his narrow escape from the dam.

The Bonneville Dam was only the first of many jobs on Northwest dams for Devine. But these repair projects were little more than distractions from his real passion for recovering lost ships. The Columbia River's wicked waves, rocks, and sandbars kept his divers from rescuing some stranded ships. He saw too many ships run aground, and the tugboats unable to reach them in time. He was often angry and felt helpless as he watched the ocean's deadly breakers quickly destroy growing numbers of good vessels. Devine hated to be reminded that the sea was stronger than his will and determination.

World War II roared through the globe with all its devastating force and every available hand was needed to help the cause. More ships passed through the Portland-Vancouver shipyards during the war than anywhere else along the Northwest coast. Devine was the salvage master on nearly every underwater job in the shipyards. Devine supervised 80 divers in the Kaiser Shipyard in Vancouver. His divers were desperately needed for underwater repair jobs on the battered ships. Still insisting on doing much of the dangerous work himself, Devine balanced diving and managing the other divers. During this time, Devine couldn't stand watching these helpless freighters being destroyed in the water and he never forgot about his plans for the perfect salvage tug. He asked the foreman at Kaiser to set aside all of his earnings in a deposit account. Not letting anyone know what his plans were, he let the money accumulate until the end of the war.

On September 2, 1945, after the surrender of Japan, Devine stayed on working at the Kaiser shipyards. He told his boss to keep his extra earnings safely in his account until he could use it to purchase a ship that fit into his plans for the perfect salvage tug. One afternoon, he had spotted a Landing Ship Medium, (LSM) which had been used to land troops and supplies overseas during the invasions. The LSM lit a spark in his mind. Its appearance reminded him of an old sketch he had made of the kind of salvage vessel he had dreamed of building many years ago. Now after his day's work was over, he would again sit at his desk with a drawing tablet sketching, revising, and then tossing his ideas into the wastebasket. Finally, he completed a set of drawings that would later become the blueprints of his salvager.

In 1948, the government was unloading much of its wartime fleet at scrap prices, far below their original costs. Devine heard about a series of LSM landing vessels that were available in San Francisco, they were 203 feet long, thirty-four feet wide, and had a draft of nine feet. He went back to his boss and told him that he intended to purchase one. Mortgaging his home, his business and using most of his savings, Devine bought the ship and spent the rest of his money converting it into his dream tug. He docked his liner at the Consolidated Builders, Inc. facilities at Swan Island, which was a Kaiser subsidiary that continued to repair and modify ships. He worked with the company to convert the liner into his vision of a salvager adding many needed features. By using his credit with the Consolidated Builders, Devine scrounged and foraged through the other vessels for much of the necessary equipment for this ship that Devine would name the *Salvage Chief.*

The Kaiser Shipyard became his playground. Converting the LSM, he installed the best surplus machinery he could find: two Fairbanks-Morse ten-cylinder engines on the lowest deck (giving his creation a total of 3,600 horsepower) and six giant electrical anchor winches driven by diesel generators mounted above the engines on the main deck. He built a storage room to hold any equipment he thought might be useful including six eight-inch electric portable pumps that could throw 9,000 gallons of water per minute, air compressors that produced 110 cubic-feet per minute, winches and cables, full gear for all the divers, fire-fighting apparatus, etc. In addition to this, he installed a complete machine shop which included underwater cutting and welding torches, lathes, drill presses, grinders, hoists, and steel plating. He changed the accommodations from sleeping up to 150 men, to 30 men.

On the aft deck, he fitted two large topping blocks from an old logging operation, amidships a massive deck crane, and on the forward deck a 12,000-pound Ellis salvage anchor. On the bridge, he placed the latest navigating apparatus—Loran and radar. He reduced the size of the sleeping quarters, leaving just enough living space for thirty divers and tenders. He had the entire deck covered in steel and welded its bow doors into place. A roller was installed on the stern floor for the mounting of a huge anchor with chains and cables. (Devine frequently used a helicopter so he added a helicopter landing pad.)

Devine's floating powerhouse was able to cruise 1,000 miles at 14 knots. It had a pull of 400 tons, equal to several large tugs. The fuel tanks could carry more than 4,100 gallons of diesel oil, enabling the *Salvage Chief* to travel great distances in the open sea. His unique system of using winch power gave the *Salvage Chief* a greater, steadier pulling ability than a propeller-driven tug. The conversion took every dime he could lay his hands on. He worked on his pet project nearly every day until nightfall. Men gathered daily to scoff at Devine's dream machine. They nicknamed it, "Devine's Scrap Heap." It was finally completed in 1949.

Devine hired an old friend, Captain Vince Miller, to oversee the operation of the *Salvage Chief*. Mrs. Devine, who had been on every major salvage job he performed, was on the shore with her two-way radio. She relayed her husband's directions from the tug to the men working along the shore. Together, they tackled jobs with a pioneering perspective, with critics sneering along the shoreline at each interval.

The *Salvage Chief's* first job was in August of 1949 when the *S.S. Pine Bluff Victory* ran aground along the Columbia River near the mouth of the Willamette River. After several other tugs had tried to refloat her, the *Salvage Chief* succeeded by using three anchors. In May of 1950, the *Salvage Chief* made local headline news by freeing the Cannery Tender, *Deneb*, with a shipment of fish boats and nets heading up north to Alaska. The *Deneb* grounded on the Long Beach Peninsula in Washington, only ten miles north of the entrance to the Columbia River. Skeptics and passersby watched as Devine set out to prove his dream machine could work. He dropped his salvage anchors and backed into position and pulled the *Deneb* free from the sand.

A lot of fishermen lost bets that afternoon as the *Salvage Chief* made maritime history rescuing a ship by backing against the waves towards deeper water. "Must have been an accident," sneered a fisherman. "Fred was just lucky."

As word spread about the *Salvage Chief's* rescue operation, Devine was busy up and down the West Coast and along its waterways. Yet, many men were still skeptical about Devine's invention and its abilities and considered its recent rescues as bizarre strokes of luck.

The Salvage Chief
Photograph by Larry Barber

Devine's luck held as he continued to gamble on salvages. He took one of his biggest risks shortly after the surrender of Japan. The salvage business was slow, so he purchased the half-sunken hull of an old Japanese cargo ship. The ship was part of a Navy-sponsored auction of 35,000 tons of scrap metal, buildings, ship pieces and construction tools left in the Aleutian Islands after the war.

Devine and his men had gone by a charter plane from Anchorage, Alaska to the tiny islands in the Aleutian chain to examine the ships and equipment up for sale. A 9,700-ton, 405-foot long Japanese troopship, the *Nozima Maru*, immediately caught his trained eye. Built in 1935, the *Nozima Maru* was one of the NKY line's best prewar freighters.

She had been used as an express between Seattle and Japan during the height of the silk market, and at the beginning of the World War II, the Japanese had converted her into a cargo transporter. Now, the lifeless vessel lay in the shallow waters off of Kiska Harbor, Alaska. Devine saw the *Nozima Maru* as an opportunity. He planned to cut her at the number three hold and get her seaworthy long enough to float her to Japan. He figured he could sell her as scrap for as much as $600,000.

Excited at the prospect of once again being a daredevil entrepreneur, Devine returned to Swan Island and began preparing the *Salvage Chief* for the journey north. Spending over $500,000, he added improvements, such as an additional 30-ton cargo boom, extra electric winches and strengthening plates. He hired an eighteen-man crew and installed a radio with a 3,000-mile radius.

"We'll have to take everything aboard," Devine said, "for we'll be a hell of a away from a store." Several months later, the *Nozima Maru* was successfully floated and was on her way to a buyer in Japan, when a violent storm hit on the high sea. The *Nozima Maru*'s seams tore open and she was lost to the sea. Devine had invested over $200,000 on his gamble and only received a portion of his money back from the insurance claims. Despite the loss, life went on.

Devine's most difficult task came with the grounding of the *Yorkmar*. On December 8, 1952, the 10,000-ton, 441-foot Liberty ship ran aground near Gray's Harbor, Washington. She was driven off course by a fierce storm that wrapped itself around the harbor. Missing the jetty, the *Yorkmar* enmeshed itself into the Washington shoreline. A huge storm pounded against her sides accompanied by the hammering of colossal surf. Within minutes, the *Yorkmar* was driven broadside into the breakers and pushed high up onto the beach. Devine's services were requested. After three years of waiting, the moment had come for the *Salvage Chief* to prove herself.

Devine stood on the bow of the deck, his legs spread wide, his aching, burned neck thrust forward, and his blue eyes scanning the mist, looking for clues to saving the *Yorkmar*. "Hell, we'll drag her in," Devine said to Captain Vince Miller. Even though the *Salvage Chief* was ready, Devine was worried. He kept thinking, "Would all of my ingenuity be able to rescue this ship anchored so firmly into the sand?"

The *Salvage Chief* powered through the waters from its station base in Astoria, Oregon but did not arrive in Gray's Harbor until three days later. High winds and raging seas prevented her from entering the port. On December 11th the men were able to get within 2,000 feet of the battered *Yorkmar*. "Damn," yelled Devine. "Can't we get any closer?" He glared at Captain Miller.

"A few feet maybe," Captain Miller bellowed back. "We've been trying for two days. We're off of the bottom now. Much more and we'll have to put wheels on the Chief." Devine scowled, "We've got to get a line aboard that ship. Then the Chief could pull her out of there - pronto. Much longer and she'll break up. I've seen it happen before - too often."[6] Devine gritted his teeth and took over. He set two of his anchors, and then he backed through the water-stern first! As the *Salvage Chief* approached the *Yorkmar*, getting as close as 1,200 feet, she was riding the breakers in only ten feet of water. Devine did not want his vessel to become stranded as well, so he ordered Captain Miller to back away from the beached ship. The men returned to explore other options.

After seven days and many attempts, the men tried to secure a line between the *Salvage Chief* and the *Yorkmar*. Each time the line was being secured, one of the *Salvage Chief's* anchor cables stretched and snapped, and the remaining anchor began to drag along the bottom. With each failed attempt, the ferocious waves through the *Salvage Chief* into the breakers again and again. Devine ordered the towline dropped and the remaining anchor's cable cut. "It'll take ten minutes to cut that cable, sir," the cable man informed Devine. "Ten minutes - hell!" yelled Devine. "We'll cut it pronto. You haul it aboard. We'll be back"[7] He then steered expertly out into deeper water and away from the breakers.

By now, the crowd along the water was taking bets on whether the *Salvage Chief* was anything more than an expensive toy. But Devine would not give up; he knew that his vessel could pull the *Yorkmar* free. Fighting both storm and sea, Devine recalculated what he believed would work and returned to port in Astoria for extra gear.

The storm had calmed a bit on Devine's return. He backed into the breakers, secured the anchors and set his towline to the *Yorkmar*. It was now on the 16th of December, when Devine floated a line from the *Salvage Chief's* deck gun onto an empty oil barrel to the shore; a Coast Guardsman was able to walk the line over the rusting, beached *Yorkmar*. The following morning, the tide rose and the *Yorkmar* pulled against the strain of the towline. Devine grasped his line tight and the *Yorkmar* moved 200 feet towards the sea. The sand held her firm, and she dug deeper into the ground. Tightening up the line, even more, Devine ordered around the clock watch on the *Yorkmar*. The storm increased overnight and on the 18th of December, a 12-foot flood of water hit the shore.

A back-up tug was called out from San Francisco to help the *Salvage Chief*. While they waited for her arrival, all eyes were on the straining line between the Salvage Chief and the *Yorkmar*. The *Sea Lion* tug arrived and was stationed west of the *Salvage Chief*. She laid her lines to the *Salvage Chief* to hold her from moving into the *Yorkmar*.

As the waves beat into the shore, Devine revved up the *Salvage Chief's* engine to more than 4,000 horsepower. That much force was necessary to free the Yorkmar from the sand. Oscar Kullbom, the ship's captain, and his crew of 36 men went back on board to start their engines to help break free when Devine gave the last mighty pull. Foot-by-foot, stern first, she crawled across the sand until she was out past the breakers. Both tugs kept their engines revved and pulled the *Yorkmar* four miles offshore. "I think that we can float her in another half ship's length," Devine estimated to Captain Miller.

Once in deep water, the *Yorkmar* could operate under her own power. After some hull repair back at the shipyard, she was ready to go back to work. Devine had rescued most of her $140,000 cargo. He had proven his worth and astonished the public by saving the *Yorkmar* from a seemingly impossible situation. No one ever doubted Devine and his dream salvage machine again.

Devine kept inventing and modifying his equipment after many successful salvages. Even before the *Salvage Chief* was in the water, Devine had invented a diving dress that could be removed while underwater. By adding detachable screws on the back of his helmet, Devine proved the outfit's reliability by diving into the Willamette River with his diving dress on, to emerge moments later wearing only a swimsuit. In 1953, Devine modified the plate glass front of his diving helmets. After having the faceplate of his helmet shatter one time while he was on the bottom, Devine began replacing the plate glass with bullet-resisting glass. He adapted several types of pneumatic-driven saws and other "hand" tools for use underwater. Devine also added hoses and air controls to the front of the shoulder on the diving dress, making for easier repairs and quick escapes from danger. To this day, salvagers around the Northwest still use his inventions.

Devine died in 1971, at age 73. After a lifetime of salvage work, he had rescued over $100 million dollars in distressed ships and cargo that would have otherwise been lost. He made key contributions to the growth of the salvage industry with advanced techniques and diving apparatus. Much of his work was strictly a gamble - from creating and modifying tools to accepting jobs on "no cure-no pay" contracts.

Today, Fred Devine Diving & Salvage Incorporation is owned and operated by The Marine Salvage Consortium, Inc., a group formed by three maritime firms. Senior Salvage Master, J.H. "Mick" Leitz, manages the company. The *Salvage Chief* has become the most famous salvage tug in the world. She provided assistance in repairing and refloating the damaged *Exxon Valdez* that beached on a rock-strewn reef in Alaska, spilling over 11 million gallons of oil in 1989. To date, she has rescued over 325 distressed vessels from the Arctic down to Mexico. Today, she is docked in Astoria, awaiting her next rescue job.

THE TOUGHEST DIVE

No diver wants to think about it: when the river swallows its victims, it is he who must descend for the recovery. Many times the bodies are trapped under pilings, rocks or the steel hull of a sunken vessel. Never is the dive more horrifying than when the body is that of the diver's own father.

Walter James McCray was born in Scotland and came to America with his family. His father had been a captain of a coal ship near Aberdeen, Scotland. When the ship struck a rock in 1885, it went down and his father drowned. Mrs. McCray would not let her husband's death keep her family in poverty. With the help of her brothers, she took her children to America. The McCray family began their new life traveling across the United States. After several months of odd work and travel, they settled near Puget Sound, Washington. Mrs. McCray's son, Walter McCray, was an eager young man with big plans to make a lot of money in America.

Diving came naturally to McCray. Burly and broad-shouldered, the young man sought exciting activities and ended up working as a salvage diver along the Washington coast and in Alaska. In 1898, while still in his early teens, McCray served as an apprentice diver. Shortly afterward, he was called to help salvage the wreck of the *S.S. Adelina*. Not one crewmember of that ill-fated vessel survived when the freighter turned over during a deadly storm. One hired salvage diver had already been crushed underneath the sunken ship when McCray was called onto the job. McCray gained valuable insight into salvage diving from the job that helped to shape his career.

When McCray turned eighteen, he set out on an English square-rigged ship, the *Springbank*. Returning home for a brief time, he volunteered his services during the Russo-Japanese War in 1903. McCray was one of the crewmembers captured while attempting to run the blockade at Port Arthur, China. After two months in a prison camp, McCray and the others were released into the waiting hands of an English warship.

McCray eventually set up his own salvage business in Tacoma. By 1905, his activities had taken him all around the country. He was quickly recognized as one of the top three salvage divers north of the Columbia River. He was well known as the diver who had single-handedly raised the entire cargo from a wrecked ship and who had at one time managed twenty-six fishing traps all on his own. The name McCray soon became synonymous with underwater explorer because of the many dangerous encounters he had survived beneath the choppy waves.

In 1927, out from a dock at Glacier Pit, near Steilacoom, Puget Sound, the 82-foot steam tug, *C.C. Cherry*, was capsized by a fully loaded grit scow, which sat between her and the dock. The scow had taken on too much sand and gravel and began tilting, spilling much of its load.

Walter McCray, 1926
Photograph from Ron McCray

The backlash from this action took the *C.C. Cherry* down with a loud whop. The tug quickly filled with water, and at the same time, the blow to her bows kicked her 180 feet out into the sound.

McCray was always ready for the impossible. Working with a derrick crane, he began the rescue of the capsized tug. As always, he did his own diving, battling deep water and a temperamental current. He speedily located the vessel seventy-five feet below the surface and was so relieved that it was undamaged, except for the oil that spilled from her fuel tanks. The *C.C. Cherry* was ready for work the following week. McCray's achievement set a salvage record for raising a sunken tug in only thirty hours. His work was mentioned in all of the newspapers around the Pacific Northwest.

Later in 1927, a Northwestern steamer arrived in the smelter docks that were so overcrowded, it anchored about a mile and a half off the docks. When the liner started to move into her berth she lost her three-ton anchor and chain. McCray was working at the smelter dock, so the men asked him to locate lost its anchor and chain. He dared the ocean by doing the impossible, diving down twenty-two fathoms off Puget Sound. Only one diver before him had attempted such a feat. William Baldwin successfully went down to the British ship *Andelana*; he lost his life on the second attempt to locate this ship.

Getting equipped for this courageous dive meant McCray had to be extra careful that all of his equipment was ready and at hand. Putting on a rubber-canvas diving dress with an outer suit that weighed around 110 pounds (50 pounds of this is just the breast weights and 20 pounds of rubber-soled shoes), McCray headed towards the water. Two of his assistants began hand pumping the compressor, while two extra men stood by ready to take over.

The men cranked the hand-powered compressor with robust determination. As the needle climbed to sixty pounds, McCray lifted his hand in a half wave to his airline tender and leaped into the water leaving only a trace of bubbles to attest to his presence. Communication was limited by a one-way telephone receiver. The tender on shore could hear McCray, but McCray could not hear the tender. His air hose was his only contact with the world above. One jerk meant "Yes," two - meant "No."

Struggling against the tide and enveloping darkness, McCray went down the 19 fathoms where the ship had been. McCray discovered that the anchor was in deeper water as the steamer had moved a bit after losing the anchor. McCray went right back down into the deep water near where he thought the anchor was, but he found out that his air hose was too short for this depth. Ascending back to the surface, taking a few feet at a time, he got more hose and went down for a third try.

Although strong sunlight sometimes reached the harbor bottom, it was barely enough to light his way. All the work had to be done using hand tools and a careful touch. Once on the bottom, the sand was smooth and the water was very clear. Fighting the deadly pressure (At the depth of 130 feet, it is about seventy pounds to the square inch, or almost 5 times the pressure felt at sea level.), McCray overcame the discomfort he felt by the weight pressing on him. McCray's weights were secured tightly across his body before descending, and when they became slack in the water his entire body felt as though it were fighting an underwater windstorm. Finally, he located the anchor on his fourth dive. McCray secured the end of a steel cable around its hook. Pulled by the *Peter Foss* Tug, the anchor lifted and was coasted into shallow water, then heaved into the mud flats at the end of the waterway.

McCray Meets a "Devil Fish"

Sometimes, the divers had more to fear than the water itself. The creatures that made their home in the murky deep also posed a threat. The octopus, or "devil fish," was the nightmare of most divers in the Northwest. Perhaps it is its hideous looks: its parrot-like beak, pinkish jelly-like body, or its beady, black eyes that peer maliciously out from behind rocks and caves. Maybe is it because they are loners, hiding from other sea life and lurking on the dark. Their eight suction-inlaid tentacles can spread out to over twenty-five feet, which can be a frightening sight for a lone diver underwater. With their long grotesque arms, they will attack anything - including divers!

McCray had encountered many an octopus while working underwater. In 1928, he was hired by Apex Fishing Company to examine one of its fish traps along Alden Banks, near Anacortes, Washington. He had made two dives and completed his evaluations, when, while checking the lead to the trap, McCray encountered the dreaded creature. He was eighty-five feet below the surface when suddenly he found himself in the deadly clutch of an enormous octopus. The unexpected attack threw McCray off balance and he toppled into the wire mesh of the snare. His air hose got tangled in the wire, holding him against the nets. The octopus squirted him with a thick, black stream of ink that obstructed his vision. In a calm voice, McCray told his lead tender, Jimmy Hill, on the scow, "Now keep cool. Don't get excited. A devil fish has got me."

When Jim heard about McCray's predicament, it made his hair stand on end. A few minutes later, McCray asked Hill to hold the scow steady to avoid putting pressure on the lifeline. McCray said that he was dangerously entangled in the web of the trap. Hill confirmed McCray's order by tugging once on the line. While McCray fought against the octopus, it threw two more strong tentacles around his exhausted body. He was wrapped from arm to groin in the slimy grip of his attacker. His left arm was crushed tightly to his side, and he felt another tentacle reaching up against his back. The large, ugly head of the monster rested on McCray's chest, its ravenous eyes boring into its alarmed victim. McCray relayed his dire situation to Hill, who was supervising the attendants. The men on the scow stood by helplessly as they listened to the imperiled diver on the one-way telephone. The men could see

McCray's lifeline being pulled and hear his heavy breathing while he tried to free himself from the octopus' lethal grip.

McCray reached down with his right arm and pulled a knife from his belt. The depth and water pressure quickly consumed his strength. After fighting fiercely for more than forty-five minutes to gain his freedom, he tried to break the inflexible grasp of the slimy arms. Worn out, McCray aimed the knife at the predator carefully, so as not to cut his airline or puncture his suit, either of which would undoubtedly have meant a quick death. Staying composed the entire time, he talked over the telephone to Hill, describing his fight as it progressed. Hill stood on the scow's edge with the telephone receiver clutched to his ear, listening to the explicit narration while McCray breathlessly fought for his life. McCray told Hill that he might not be able to free himself. Finally, Hill heard, "I've got him." "No, he still has me." More gasps for air came over the telephone line. "I don't know whether I will get out of this or not; the old sport won't let go." Silence followed.

After numerous attempts, McCray managed to cut the tentacle free from between his legs. He continued stabbing at the beast until it finally relaxed its hold long enough for McCray to partially free himself. McCray had to cut yards of netting away in order to untangle his line from the fish trap wire. All the while, the octopus had an aggressive grip on the diver's left arm and leg.

Once free from the steel grid, McCray gave four tugs on his airline, signaling his men to bring him to the surface. "Be careful of my air," McCray said as he ascended, still in the clutches of the octopus. Now out of the water, the sea monster finally released its strangling grip and fell back. Fatigued and quite shaken, McCray attempted to climb the ladder to the scow, but he was so weary that he fell back into the water and had to be helped on board by his men. A few minutes after removing his helmet, he started to regain his strength.

The dying octopus was dragged on board with a pike pole. It had eleven knife wounds puncturing its body. When the men laid it out to measure its length, the arms stretched over nine feet. What surprised the men the most was that McCray had taken his knife with him on the dive. Having just a few hours earlier gone down to prove that the traps weren't tight, he caught a salmon on his knife and brought it up on board. Tossing the knife and fish on the barge, he descended for a second time. It was on his third dive that day that one of the tenders suggested that he take his knife along and snag another salmon. If McCray had not taken his knife, the octopus would have crushed him. Two days later, McCray was back on the job in spite of the harrowing experience and the brutal beating his body had taken.

McCray's Final Dive

The morning was especially clear for October, and McCray had secured his diving dress and helmet for his descent into the Chehalis River at Aberdeen, Washington. Adjusting his air hose, he signaled to his tender as he sank beneath the surface. While descending, McCray may have reflected on the extensive interview he gave to a Seattle paper that week, marking his thirty years in the diving business.

Diving in Gray's Harbor had become all too familiar. Over the years, McCray had recovered over a dozen bodies from these perilous waters. So many cars had driven over the railings, plunging passengers to their deaths. Once, when a ferry scow carrying the contents of a carnival sank, McCray had the unpleasant job of bringing up cages of drowned alligators and snakes in this very bay. The blank stares of the dead reptiles only served to remind him of the numerous bodies he had recovered. His mind may even have wandered back a year ago to his very own brush with death in this river.

Working back in the fall of 1933 near the Oregon-Washington railway bridge, McCray was repairing a pipeline in shallow waters. While he was under, a tugboat crashed into his barge, the *Diver I*. The collision knocked his two tenders off of their feet, leaving his hand air pump unattended. McCray's airflow suddenly stopped, and the water pressure began to close in on him. Luck was on his side, and he pulled out of the water only seconds before collapsing. Now, one year later, he was on the Chehalis again. It didn't worry him a bit; it was just another routine job.

On the morning of October 26, 1934, McCray and his son, Walter Arthur McCray, were busy diving and repairing together, making the best father and son team around Washington State. McCray was proud of his son's work, having trained him for construction diving from the time he was a young teen. Senior McCray had taken his son out on the water on his fifteenth birthday in 1930. He watched as the young boy suited up in his diving dress, then sent him down in twenty-five feet of Puget Sound water. From then on, "Art" was his father's shadow.

In August of 1934, Art, only nineteen years old, got his first independent diving job working in the wintry waters of Wrangell Narrows, Alaska. The request came from the naval base in Dutch Harbor, Alaska. The Tuscarora reef had been destroying ships since before the Russians had sold Alaska to the United States. The reef had to be cleared for the proposed Naval Base. 1,200 cubic yards of rock had to be blasted out of Dutch Harbor. He spent four months diving below the icy waters enlarging a ship channel. Art, always the inventor as well as the contractor, developed a wagon drill to be used underwater. He also re-rerouted the exhaust from the drill because the divers underwater could not stand the noise of the drilling.

Art had just returned the week before the new Chehalis River job began, ready and able to work with his father, as a professional diver. They had been laying submarine water mains for the City Water Department of Aberdeen for the past three months. The pipe and the timbers that were to be bolted over the main were nearly all laid when Walt McCray went down for his final dive of the day. The muddy water made his visibility poor. All the pilings had been cut off using a crosscut saw (called a "Misery Whip") and drilled with a compressed air drill. The pilings were the base for the water pipe, which is carefully set, one length at a time. They were only fifteen days away from completing their work, as the ten-foot ditch for the main had already been dredged and the pilings were set in the trench.

The water was cold and muddy. Fighting the tangled lines and air hose, McCray descended fifty feet down. He had been working in the trench for about two hours of a five-hour shift when he gave an emergency tug on his line and telephoned his men to pull him out of the water. That was the last the tender heard from McCray: the telephone had gone dead. Several attempts were made to bring him up from below, but each time his lifeline tightened around unseen entanglements. The men pulled and pulled on the line, but it stiffened each time, holding their diver fast on the bottom. The surface looked eerily calm; McCray was apparently tangled in the mud below. Fearing that they might break the airline, the men stopped tugging and decided someone needed to go down after him.

Arthur McCray had gone into town for lunch. Men were sent to find him to tell him of the emergency. W.J. Rogers, a veteran diver from Hoquiam, Washington, offered to go down and help McCray. Arthur was very much like his father and was determined to go down himself. Arthur donned his gear and went below. Following the trail of air bubbles coming from the unbroken line, Arthur quickly surveyed the area where his father had been working. The water was so murky that his first plunge was unsuccessful. After a second dive, Arthur reached his father's body. It was partially submerged in a cave-in along the muddy bottom. His eyes fell on a log stump that apparently had cut loose from an old string of logs near the fifteen-foot ditch where they had been working. The stump had struck the senior McCray in the head, loosening his metal helmet just enough for water to cascade into his suit drowning him. The heavy breastplate had been smashed and possibly his air ballast had collapsed as well.

Arthur wrapped his arms around his father and signaled the tender to pull them up. At first, Arthur came up alone, collapsing on the edge of the barge, and then catching his breath for a moment, he then fell back into the water. On his return to the surface, he held his father's body, the helmet broken and dangling off, his head slumped on the mangled uniform. As more than 500 people gathered along the West Bridge to watch the rescue, Arthur brought his father's body out of the water and gently placed it on the barge. More than an hour had passed by since his father had last signaled for help. The Aberdeen fire department was ready nearby. An attempt was made to resuscitate the diver, but it was no use. Walter McCray died from the collapse of his chest and shoulders - crushed by some object in the water below.

Arthur was shattered. He was too weak to stand and sat sobbing on the barge's edge. Grief-stricken, he went home to his mother and two sisters to tell them the terrible news. Having learned from his father that a dive job must get done on time, Arthur returned to the site and finished the job that the father and son team had been working on together.

After thirty-five years of diving, Walter McCray was fifty years old when he was crushed to death by a cave-in fifty feet below the surface of the Chehalis River in Aberdeen. The following Saturday, one of the largest gatherings of divers, including Captain Henry Finch, met at Pier 40 in Seattle to pay their last respects to their colleague. When Arthur McCray took over his father's business, his name and his work became known, just like his father's, throughout the Pacific Northwest.

ART MCCRAY: THE LEGEND CONTINUES

Walter McCray instructed his son, Walter Arthur McCray, in the ways of diving. When most boys were learning to toss a football, Arthur could calculate the pressure at specific depths, operate the lines and hoses and regulate an air gauge. He spent four years under his father's masterful guidance.

In 1934, there was no insurance coverage available to cover the life and health of a diver. When the senior McCray drowned, his family was granted the minimum allotment of $13.00 for their loss. The money made a mockery of the life of a father and one of the finest divers in the Northwest. The McCray Co. of Seattle had lost its founder but gained a new proprietor in the salvage market: the undaunted nineteen-year-old, Art McCray. With five hundred dollars, borrowed from his mother, he kept the McCray Co. alive; the business was the only means of keeping the McCray family afloat. Although it was troubling walking the same waterfront his father had while looking for work, McCray would not quit. McCray quickly proved that he was as honest as his father had been. He soon learned by trial and error how to competitively bid on work, and found out how to handle each job as he went under. Worry and tough work often turned seeming losses into profits.

McCray nearly lost his life while working along the same waterline as his father. He remembered how only two weeks before he had to go down in the water to bring his father's lifeless body back to the barge. When he found his father, he had been buried in mud. Now, as McCray was lying on his side next to the waterline, he soon realized that mud was beginning to cover him. He notified his tenders and the men on the barge sent down a siphon to remove the heavy clay. As more mud heaped across his body, McCray crawled away from his work site and had his tenders pull him up. After catching his breath, he went back down, only to discover that his tools had been buried.

On November 7, 1940, the Tacoma Narrows Bridge, the third longest suspension span bridge in the world, collapsed due to its design. Located on the Tacoma Narrows in Puget Sound, near the city of Tacoma, Washington, the bridge had only been open for travel a few months. The strong Pacific Ocean winds buckled the bridge and the entire deck fell to the bottom of the Sound. (Parts of the original bridge still lay there today.) McCray was called upon to repair the bridge from the footing of the pilings to the tip of the fallen towers. The underwater structure had to be salvaged and rebuilt. Work was made more difficult by the fast current, such that McCray couldn't stand upright underwater: his legs remained parallel with the surface.

By the end of 1940, McCray had the best-equipped diving barge on the west coast. McCray designed the *Diver III* to be eighteen feet wide, fifty-six feet long with a small house on it. It was built to accommodate the divers while away on a job.

Art McCray, 1953
Photograph from Ron McCray

The comforts included three bunks, a full galley and the latest equipment available, including a 75-horsepower engine (equal to 15 lawnmower engines) and a compression chamber, one of the first to be commercially used on this coast. The heavy steel chamber provided enough room for a diver to rest comfortably on a bunk while decompressing on the barge. The use of the chamber meant a diver no longer had to rely on nature to pass the nitrogen out of his system. The hours saved using this mechanical decompression process meant less time spent idle between dives. The chamber also proved much safer for a diver that needed to be pulled out of an underwater emergency.

1940 was a good year for McCray. Not only was he the owner of the largest diving company in Seattle, but he also set record dives in the cool waters of the Grand Coulee Dam. While under contract with the Bureau of Reclamation, McCray dived to the depth of 235 feet several times, searching for a stop-log steel grating lost during construction. Much of McCray's success can be credited to his ingenuity and talent for invention. In 1942, McCray perfected his diver hat while he and his companions were working overtime during World War II.

The Diver III
Photograph from Rom McCray

As most diving helmets were large and cumbersome, they could keep a diver from getting into small places underwater. Often, not being able to get his head close to his work restricted a diver's visibility. Sometimes a diver had to use weights to sink his helmet in the water since these large standard helmets were also buoyant when they were filled with air. These helmets also made any work a diver did difficult because he had to keep fighting just to keep the helmet from rising to the surface.

Growing tired of these bulky helmets, McCray modified his old Mark V naval helmet by shrinking the space of the helmet dome. By doing this, McCray's new helmet weighed less, so he could lighten his weight belt by 10-20 pounds. The smaller dome gave the helmet neutral buoyancy underwater, so he no longer had to fight to keep his helmet down in the water. McCray could now comfortably work in horizontal positions, get closer to his work and move much more freely in the water. He then put the head valve at the back of the dome and connected the telephone lines inside the helmet, rather than on the shoulder. He raised the neck ring and moved the airline to fit directly under the diver's nose, with the exhaust valve in the back. Morse Helmet Company made the design but felt that the helmets would be too small for most divers' heads. The design never reached commercial fame; however, it led many divers around the Northwest to modify their own helmets into "McCray" hats.

McCray relentlessly took on the challenges of diving as he traveled all around the United States. In one week he went from the Boeing airfield in Seattle to "blow out" sand in the sewer, to being called to Cody, Wyoming to work on the Shoshone Dam. Diving for lost warships in Alaska often took him down below the safety of the 200-depth mark. McCray had to learn to keep his eyes shut on his descent to the bottom because the extreme depth could make him lose his sense of balance. The mind plays tricks on a diver deep in the water. Confusion or loss of concentration can become the diver's worst enemy.

In 1941, the War Shipping Administration asked McCray to supervise the removal of two huge boulders, over thirty tons of rock, in Sitka Harbor, Alaska. The *S.S. Dorothy Alexander* had struck them while attempting to anchor at the harbor. The boulders, one of which weighed as much as 20 tons, were firmly in the floor of the harbor. At low tide, they jutted out only about eight feet above the water, so a large ship could not see them until it was too late. Diving from a scow, McCray attached several steel cables around the smaller boulder and he managed to get the ten-ton rock to rise to the surface. The heavier boulder was more of a challenge for McCray. After four attempts of using cables and winches all around it, the boulder did not budge. The cables snapped like ribbons into the water. McCray would not give up, on his fifth try he succeeded. Both rocks were taken out past the harbor and dumped in deeper water. The War Department was so pleased with his work, McCray was kept on call for other shipping contracts.

Ron McCray, 3rd generation McCray diver
Photograph from Ron McCray

One of the most frightening jobs McCray undertook involved a submerged Japanese ship, which supposedly had time bomb still on board. McCray was to go down and safely retrieve the bomb. Demolition experts had mistakenly reported the bomb harmless just two minutes before they heard the buzzing of the bomb's setting. McCray was already on the bottom recovering it from under a pier! Fortunately for McCray, the bomb was broken.

In 1945, McCray dived in over 215 feet of water, trying to salvage an eighty-foot wooden minesweeper YP-83. A Navy torpedo plane had struck the ship by accident in the Saratoga Passage three miles off Whidbey Island in Washington. He purchased the vessel "as is" and planned on making it into a fishing boat. McCray went down to the sweeper thirty times, examining the damage to her starboard side and placing steel cables under her. A one hundred ton lifter was used to tow her into shallow water. After retrieving the damaged minesweeper, McCray temporarily patched it before sending it to the Ballard Marine Railway Company's yard for dry docking and to repair the hole in her starboard bow.

Good work brought in top pay. McCray revamped the *Diver III* with a fresh coat of bright red paint, several top of the line canvas diving outfits (even then, the canvas usually broke down under use within six months to a year) built a new $300,000 crane named the Bolwar SS and put in a new engine.

Spike and Ron, two of McCray's sons, worked under his paternal guidance as commercial divers. Although McCray rarely ever mentioned the horror of finding his own father's body in the Chehalis River, he never allowed his own sons to dive there. By McCray's fifty-fifth birthday, he quit diving fulltime and was ready to retire after forty years in the business. He did well when he invested $3,200 into his father's business after the senior McCray's death: the company was now worth more than $1 million.

Dick Pegg bought out McCray's business in 1967. He was the head of a group known as the Garrison 8 Divers, who had made a name for themselves both in construction and underwater work. They kept the name, McCray Marine Construction Company, and Arthur was consulted on various marine construction jobs throughout the Northwest.

To this day, Spike McCray, Ron McCray, and Ron's daughter, Tammy, dive for pleasure. Ron is in charge of underwater construction for a marine construction firm. His youngest son, Steve, chose not to dive; he became a flyer. Dave Clark, one of the original Garrison 8 Divers still used the *Diver III* in his own diving company until he retired.

GUESTS OF THE EMPEROR

When Robert Sheats enlisted in the military in November of 1941, he had no idea that months later he would be a witness to the Japanese bombing of the Cavite Navy Yard in the Philippines. At the age of twenty-six, Sheats was trained as a gunner and deep-sea diver for the U.S. Navy. When captured by the Japanese, diving saved his life during the battles between the Japanese and Americans in Manila Bay. (Excerpts are from Mr. Sheats personal diary.)

The crew of the *USS Canopus,* a submarine rescue vessel, fitted with deep-sea diving uniforms and other equipment for salvaging and rescuing submarines in trouble, was stationed at the mouth of the Marivelles Harbor on the Bataan Peninsula in the Philippines. They were anchored 1000 yards offshore from the Cavite Naval Station in Manila Bay, stranded out in Chinese waters in the line of fire from the Japanese. Sheats was one of the men on the *Canopus* serving as a submarine tender.

With the Japanese bombing of Pearl Harbor on December 7, 1941, the Navy pulled every major naval vessel out of Manila Bay, except the *Canopus.* As the crew was getting low on food and they were out of ammunition and supplies, the Bataan Peninsula was being overrun by the invading Japanese army. In April of 1942, the crew of the *Canopus* salvaged deck guns, munitions, and other tools from the base before they escaped in *Canopus'* small boats to the fortress island of Corregidor in the mouth of Manila Bay. While sailing off to safety, Sheats looked back over his shoulder towards the channel. He saw the tunnel where they had hidden the remaining dynamite explode. Shards of rock and boulders flew into the air, showering the men with deadly debris. Two men were instantly killed, while the others wrapped their heads in their arms and crouched, praying for protection.

Landing at Corregidor, able men carried the wounded to a nearby emergency shelter. Leaving their comrades in safe hands, the men began a five-mile hike to their destination. Bombs continued to rain down, causing the men to scatter. Sheats and a few others ran into a culvert for safety. Keeping clear of danger, the men scurried along. Sheats and the remaining men made it to James Ravine, where they shoveled and sandbagged the area in order to keep the enemy at bay. The Canopus' crew then joined the Fourth Marine Division in beach defense.

During the fighting at Corregidor, both the Army and Naval commands dumped excess materials that might have benefited the Japanese troops into the ocean. Much of the gold and silver bullion had already been shipped out on the *USS Trout,* an American submarine. Fearing a possible surrender to the Japanese, the men were ordered to bury the remaining fifteen million pesos in silver: worth more than eight million dollars. Fortunately, the divers had managed to take navigational cross-bearings of the dumpsite.

U.S. Naval photo of Robert Sheats, February 1962
Photograph from Herman Kunz

They hid the 350 tons of silver in wooden boxes that were then dumped into the sea near the fortified islands of Corregidor and Fort Hughes. The boxes were 24x14x14 inches in size and were each filled with six thousand pesos, weighing 300 pounds each.

Diary Entry: "We went past our 200th air raid today. Our rations are getting skimpy, with only cracked wheat for breakfast. We are beginning to wonder whether the hunger or the enemy will get us first. We talk at night to bolster our courage, wondering when the attack will come. Some think in the dark of the moon, some during the full moon. I think an attack will come, but they'll lose more men than they will take, even if 'the rock' {Corregidor Island} isn't as well fortified as we thought."

After another month, on May 6, 1942, with over 10,000 shells falling on Corregidor in one 24-hour period, Sheats and his company surrendered along with the rest of the men in Corregidor. It was the only way to help the wounded and nurses who were trapped in the tunnels. The men were taken out of James Tunnel to the 92nd garage area to wait out their fate along with more than 7,000 service men and 2,500 Filipino prisoners. Marching to the step of their Japanese captors, the men passed along the sharp cliffs outside the Malinta Tunnel. Sheats looked into the eyes of the hundreds of prisoners and dying men left behind. Many of these men jumped off cliffs to their deaths rather than face the horrendous march to the prison camps.

After three weeks, the Corregidor POWs were put on freighters and sent to Manila. The men were forced to march through the streets in a Japanese victory parade to Bilibid Prison. Bilibid was an old, abandoned military prison in Manila. (Many *Canopus* sailors were kept at Bilibid for the entire wartime period.)

Diary entry on May 25th: "I left with a group of 2,000 prisoners for Nueva Ecija, Cabanatuan at 0500 hrs. We were marched to a train station and 150 loaded into each boxcar like cattle. Eleven horrible hours later we pulled into Cabanatuan. We were marched 20 kilometers to an old Philippine Army camp which had some rickety barracks for protection from the sun and wind."

Diseases were taking their toll on the men, and Sheats was soon battling jaundice and dysentery. During his recovery, he heard the Japanese announce that they were looking for deep-sea divers to return to Corregidor for salvage work. They had collected the names and rates of the divers who were captured from the USS *Pigeon* and USS *Canopus*. Too sick to go with the first call, Sheats went with the second set of divers forced to move from the prisons into enemy waters under the supervision of the Japanese.

The Japanese quickly discovered the buried silver booty. Before using the American divers to retrieve the treasure, the Japanese hired eight Filipinos to complete the task. These poor men were inexperienced at deep-sea-diving procedures. They were ignorant of decompression techniques and came up from the deep water with headaches, fatigue and the bends. Because the Japanese officers were unfamiliar with the effects of rapid decompression, the divers were only given a short rest before descending again. The agonizing deaths of two divers and little silver recovered forced all but one Filipino diver to quit.

The remaining diver, tempted by the sizable bonus, planned a different approach to the bottom. Because two divers had been killed by the bends, he figured that there was not enough air getting into the diving dress. He attempted to dive with only a Morse shallow water helmet. (This helmet is manufactured out of spun copper and rests on the diver's head much like a diving bell. Air is supplied through a gooseneck fitting on the top of the helmet and exhausts at the shoulder level.) He successfully retrieved a few boxes of silver by using the Morse helmet. The other divers, seeing his spoils, quickly put on their dive outfits, all ready to return to work. As they approached the dive platform, calamity struck again. The tender on the barge felt four yanks on the airline, signaling that the diver was ready to come up. He pulled on the air hose but only the helmet rose to the surface. The diver had forgotten to wrap the air hose under his arm to prevent the helmet from being accidentally pulled off. The remaining divers got in their boat and left the barge. Only eighteen boxes of silver had been recovered and already three people had died.

The Japanese called upon the American divers to take over the job. The water depth at the dumpsite was 120 feet. Well aware of the danger, the Japanese ordered their prisoners to dive for them. The divers were placed under Japanese salvage masters and sent out on a native flat-bottom barge called a Casco. It was rigged with a diving platform, outmoded hose, and an old U.S. Navy MK-III manually operated dive pump. This air pump was not made to operate below ninety feet of water and was inadequate for the job at hand. The divers were allowed to go aboard bombed out ships and scout for newer diving equipment. They came back with a useable hose, dive underwear and non-return valves, and then spent nearly two weeks overhauling the gear and organizing the dive operation.

On July 8, they made their first dive. The eager Filipino divers returned as tenders and pump hands. The first American diver went down to scout out the situation. Even with the rapid pumping of the hand compressor, there was barely enough air to keep his chin dry. With every inhalation, the water rose a bit higher in his helmet. The diver was unable to bend at all, for fear of getting a face full of water. Surveying the bottom, the diver easily located the wooden boxes. Most of them sat neatly stacked in a huge pile. The diver connected a lifting wire to one of the boxes and then signaled to be brought up. (Since all of the diver's personal belongings had been requisitioned at the prison, all decompression tables had been lost. The divers had to figure out the correct decompression levels from memory. They all decided to decompress for five minutes at twenty feet, and seven minutes at ten feet.)

Pleased with his work, the Japanese salvage master gave the American a bottle of Scotch whiskey. Four wooden boxes of silver pesos were secured on the first day. When Sheats was well enough, he joined these men in the salvage operation. He had a diving manual in his possession that he had hidden from the guards at the camp.

Although the decompression tables were outdated, it was well received by the men. By the time Sheats arrived, twenty-eight boxes of silver had been reclaimed.

Diary Entry: "Rather than call ourselves POWs, we coined the euphemism, 'Guests of the Emperor'."

Sheats and eight other divers were forced to continue salvaging along Corregidor for the lost silver. Working under these conditions made them feel unsure of their own success. They did not want to be retrieving silver for the enemy, yet it meant staying alive another day. As a group, the men decided to work efficiently, but slowly. Often, they fooled the Kempe Tai, the military police, who oversaw the diving operations. The divers could cancel a day's worth of diving by convincing the Kempe Tai that the tides were too strong, or that the visibility was too clouded.

In addition to the difficulty of locating the scattered wooden boxes, many of them were broken down from the salt water. It did not take much effort for the divers to occasionally "sabotage" the ends of these boxes, thus dropping much of the silver before it surfaced. The divers smuggled a small pointed tool underwater to break open the containers, which they did on days when their schedules didn't include a recovery. The divers would also smuggle silver aboard which they later used to buy extra provisions because their scanty food rations were barely enough to keep them in good physical shape for the dives. Smuggling the silver was an ingenious operation in which all the divers took part. Typical smuggling would go as follows:

The descending diver would hide a loot bag (made from a pair of old dungaree pant legs, an old gas mask bag and a strap from an old dive mask) under his dive underwear. He would then put on an old pair of tennis shoes and walk over to the ladder on the barge. There, he would check the helmet's non-return valve to be sure it was working. After the helmet had been lowered over his head, another tender would hand the diver the loop end of the 3/16-inch recovery cable. As the diver descended, he would check to be sure that the hired Filipino tender was pumping the hand compressor for his air supply and that a buddy was operating the air hose.

Sliding down the descending line, the diver signaled two pulls on the air hose for more slack. Once on the bottom, he attached the loop of the cable around a crate and signaled three pulls on the recovery wire for the tender to take up the slack. Then, using the spiked tool that had been concealed on the end of the descending line, he would open a different box and fill up his loot bag with about five hundred pesos. The loot bag would go over his shoulder, freeing his hands for the climb up the descending wire.

After securing the air hose under his arm to prevent the helmet from being tugged off, four pulls signaled the tender to begin hauling him up. Stopping at the thirty-foot level to decompress, the diver would signal ten pulls on the air hose that meant, "I have a bag of silver." Ten tugs back from the other diver meant that the coast was clear. If no tugs from the tender were returned, the diver would know to dump the bag of silver. The loot bag was then attached to another line and weighted with a snap on the end of it. This line was secretly dropped from the other side of the barge from where the wooden boxes were pulled aboard. Sheats would enter the water, pretending to go and make sure that the diver's air hose was clear of the ascending box of silver. Once under the barge, he swam to the side of the barge with the hidden line and snap, grabbed the line and took it over to the diver. The diver would secure the loot bag on the snap and let it swing free.

Back on the barge while the carton was being hauled up, one of the divers slipped to the other side and hauled up the bag of silver. It was hidden in a bucket covered by the dive underwear. The hardest part was carrying the heavy loot while walking like the bucket only contained underwear! The divers hid their treasure on board until they returned to Corregidor. On the island, they had free run of the area. By scouting and snooping, the divers found muriatic acid and wire brushes for cleaning their silver. The coins were then sent through secret channels back to the prison camp.

The Japanese salvage master's lack of knowledge increased the already high risk of the job. Although the Japanese sometimes relied on the American divers' advice and experience, often they overlooked life-threatening situations. Once, when Sheats was decompressing at the thirty-foot level, his airline and lifeline became fouled. The tender didn't notice and pulled on the airline during his ascent. This caused the Morse helmet to shake loose from Sheats' head. Although he had the air hose wrapped under his arm, the jolt knocked the helmet off of his head. Untangling himself from the helmet, Sheats began a mad swim towards the surface. As he neared the light, he could feel his lungs expanding from the air inside. Quickly, he let out all of his air. The negative buoyancy made his final ascent nearly impossible. A little sick, he made it onto the barge without serious injury.

On days off, the divers were left to their own amusements. The unspoken agreement between the Japanese sentry and the divers was that they could be left alone as long as their salvage dives that day had been successful. The Japanese had not discovered much of the island's secret supplies. Nightly search parties brought back illegal items, such as guns and ammunition, typewriters and tools that the divers hid in their quarters.

Aboard the Casco life was a different story. Preparations had been made for fear that the Japanese should decide to inspect the barge. Having been tipped off a day ahead of a surprise inspection for contraband, the men hid all silver, smuggled guns and ammunition in old ammunition cans to be retrieved later. Shortly after their last surprise inspection, the Japanese added a crew of native divers. They were from the island of Mindanao and were experienced deep-sea pearl divers. These Moro divers were well paid and had better equipment than Sheats' crew. Their barge had a British Siebe Gorman dive dress and helmet and a three-cylinder single-acting hand pump with a larger capacity than the small Filipino hand pump. The Moros knew how to decompress and were aware of the dangers involved in deep sea diving.

Robert Sheats
Photograph from Herman Kunz

Because of the incentive of high pay for outdoing the American divers, the Moros were able to retrieve the silver more quickly.

On September 29, 1942, the weather soured and both groups of divers were taken on fishing boats to Manila. After the storm, the Moro divers returned for a short while to continue the salvage work, and American divers were taken from Corregidor to a shallow part of Manila Bay later that November. They were instructed to inspect a submerged ship to determine if it could be raised.

Being forced to dive for American silver was tolerable in order to stay alive, but taking part in raising a ship that would be used against their own country was too much for any of the divers. They refused to reveal what they found and were taken across the Bay to another salvageable craft. Again, the divers went down to look but refused to comment on its condition. All of the divers were then demoted to pump hands for the Filipino divers who volunteered to raise the sunken war crafts.

For the next two and a half months, the Americans turned the pump handles for the Filipino divers. The privileged status of diving was stripped and their food was meagerly rationed as the Americans held fast to their patriotism. No matter how hard they tried, the Filipino divers were unable to raise any ships. Over six months had gone by since Sheats had been imprisoned during the battle on Corregidor. Most of this time had been spent recovering silver pesos, and secretly sabotaging the Japanese salvaging projects, all under the life-threatening orders of his captors. Now, the nine divers were again ordered to raise the vessels and the tedious job of tending the Filipinos came to an end. They still refused to inspect and repair ships for the enemy. Because of their insubordination, the men were all moved to primitive prison camps and were overworked under terrible conditions, while waiting for the war to end.

At the end of the war, only eight divers remained alive and they returned to the Pacific Northwest and California. Several attempts to salvage the silver had been undertaken by the Philippines since 1946. Although some crates were found, there still lies an abundance of blackened silver deep in the muddy waters between Corregidor and Fort Hughes. Sheats continued to work for the Navy out of the Bremerton Naval base in Washington until his retirement.

FROM DIVER TO WRITER: WALT MOREY

The author of over a dozen books for children and several articles and stories for adults, including the book, North To Danger, Walt Morey began gathering his stories while deep sea diving in Prince William Sound, Alaska. All of his stories are based on his own experiences and those of his lifelong friend, Virgil Burford. The time he and his friend spent in Alaska became the inspiration for several of Morey's future juvenile fiction books. Even the Kodiak brown bear, which moved him to write, Gentle Ben, was a real bear he saw while inspecting fish traps near Cordova, Alaska. (As told to me by Walt's wife, Peggy Morey, and taken from his early writings.)

Walt Morey was born February 3, 1907, in Hoquiam, Washington. When he was five, the family moved to Jasper, Oregon, and stayed there until he was eight years old. With not much more than a post office, Jasper was a small town scattered along the Willamette River. Having no books to read at home, the school was always a foreign, unpleasant place where Morey had to attend. Even though Morey went to a small diligent schoolhouse, he struggled with teacher-taught writing. When his family moved back to Hoquiam, Washington, the teachers at Hoquiam Elementary placed this uneducated eight-year-old in the first grade! A year later the family moved to Great Falls, Montana. Teachers pulled Morey along year-by-year and by the time he was thirteen years old, he was beginning to like reading and writing. When Morey did express himself in his own style and imagination, his writing stood on its own. Later, the family moved to Canada, living there for a year and a half. When Morey turned fifteen, the family moved again, this time to Portland, Oregon.

The Portland city schools offered more programs for Morey. He was now fifteen and in the eighth grade. In his classroom, he met a smart, sweet girl, Rosalind Ogden. They had both been born in Hoquiam, Washington, so they had a lot to share with each other. Over the years, they remained friends in school. High school was the same story for Morey, he skimped by in every class. One wonderful thing did happen for Morey in his senior year, he finally got up the nerve to ask Rosalind out on a date. After the football party they attended, they began dating and later that year, planned on getting married after graduation. Even with Rosalind's help, Morey barely graduated in June of 1926. Rosalind went off to study education in college, while Morey took a job in the sawmill. During those years, Morey kept his sawmill work, but also found a fascination with writing. At twenty years old, he began writing a novel. Now, he knew the value of reading and writing and began searching for ways to finally learn proper English.

Rosalind graduated from college and began teaching. In 1934, in the middle of the depression, they got married and began building a stable home life. In that same year, Morey published a series of stories on boxing. Over the next seven years, he kept working and writing while Rosalind taught English at the local school.

The Second World War had been going on for a while, and after the bombing of Pearl Harbor, Morey tried to enlist. At thirty-five, he was too old to serve, so he took a job at the Kaiser Shipyard, where they built baby flattops (aircraft carriers). With his experiences at the shipyard, Morey kept writing. In 1945, he had one complete manuscript, "No Cheers, No Glory", a sixty-thousand-word novel which he sold to Blue Book magazine. After that, almost everything Morey wrote he sold to magazines all around the northwest.

In 1950, while looking for a home for his in-laws, Morey met Virgil Burford. Burford was a true voyager, the type of character you would find in an old Jack London tale. Over the last twenty years, he had worked as a professional boxer, diver, fish pirate and explorer scouting out wildlife in Alaska. Morey immediately noticed the stack of air hoses, hardhat, diving tools and canvas wetsuit Burford had scattered about his den. After a slew of questions, he learned that Burford was deep-sea diving, doing seasonal work in Alaska inspecting underwater salmon traps. (Although fish traps were illegal in the United States, Alaska, not yet a state, did not enforce the fish trap laws.) Their immediate friendship not only sold Burford's house but also created a partnership, which was to last until Burford's disappearance on a fishing boat that overturned in a storm off of Prince William Sound, Alaska, in 1969. (Burford's body was never recovered.)

Burford told Morey about his first dive, which was in the cold, murky waters off Prince Island Sound, Alaska in 1939. He described the sickening smell of vinegar that assaulted his nose as he sat nervously on the dock fearing the foreman's final call. Burford had wondered how he had convinced the superintendent that he was already a diver. After all, hadn't he just watched the first diver he'd ever seen from the deck of a boat only a few days earlier? Checking all of his equipment for the twelfth time, he tried to visualize the diving dress worn by the diver he saw yesterday. The airline, telephone line, lifeline, weight belt tight, and his helmet lights "defogged" with vinegar, he was set. Running his hands over the rubber canvas dress, he checked to make sure that the helmet was locked onto the collar, and that his chin valve was opening and closing. Burford tried to remember every step that he had seen the other diver take before signaling his own attendants. He pointed to his straps and had both crewmen pull them as tight as they could. One of the men screwed Burford's faceplate shut. This imposter diver stood there feeling the weight of his gear, all two hundred pounds of it. He glanced nervously down at the treacherous water. He only had to plunge down thirty feet to locate the subterranean passage, which led from the ammunition room to the naval air base. It should be easy, he thought as he listened to the rhythmic clanking of the compressor ring through his helmet. Panic rose in his throat and he toyed with the air valve. Signaling the airline tender, Burford stepped off the barge, splashing into the water. As he floated up towards the surface, he adjusted his chin valve with his jaw to lower himself to the bottom of the sea.

The chill of the Alaskan waters rushed through his bulky dress, leaving him bitter cold. He soon discovered that walking around on the bottom of the ocean was more difficult than he had anticipated. Burford realized that increasing the air supply in his helmet eased the straining pressure against his body. When he landed on the bottom, he was within feet of the subterranean passage. Fish swam right up to his facemask, and all kinds of creatures scurried and glided along the sandy floor. He surveyed the peaks and valleys that the harsh ocean tides had created over time. He had entered a new world, seen only by a handful of people who risked their lives to explore the vast mysteries that lay beneath the sea. Lost in fascination with this new realm, Burford forgot why he was there. The voice of the tender blurting into his helmet brought him back to reality. Yes, he had located the subterranean passage. Burford wanted more time for his first look at life under the water's surface. Finally, after filling his eyes with the splendor of the sea a moment longer, he ordered the tender to haul him up.

All winter the men exchanged stories and Burford explained to Morey the mechanics of deep sea diving. Morey jumped on the chance to write about Burford's life. He soon began publishing articles about Alaska, by Virgil Burford as told to Walt Morey. The stories sold as fast as Morey could write them.

The following spring came around and Burford invited Morey to join him on a diving excursion in Cordova. He would pay him a hundred dollars for every trap he inspected. They flew up to Seattle to catch the freighter to Anchorage, where they waited for a bush pilot who would fly them to Cordova. (The most difficult part of the journey was convincing the dive master that they BOTH were skilled divers!)

Landing in Prince William Sound, Morey was in awe of the rugged beauty of the Alaskan coast. Prince William Sound stretched broadly out into the Pacific Ocean, bordered by snow-capped mountains, dotted with glaciers. It was the kind of picture he had seen only in magazines and had dreamed about when he was a boy growing up in Washington. Now he had arrived at the last frontier left for an American explorer.

Cordova was a typical Alaskan fishing town. Beyond the saltwater and kelp beds was a peculiar charm that could only be found in such places. Old speakeasies and weathered fishermen crowded the worn muddy streets framed with wooden sidewalks. Like most small coastal villages, fishing boats and men flocked to Cordova in the spring and summer. The salmon were plentiful and the canneries were operating at full speed.

Morey had only two weeks to learn how to dive. Burford arranged a ride for them on a cannery boat and took Morey out to a secluded cove to make his first dive. Peering over the edge at the murky cold water, Morey thought of the many near-death experiences that Burford had described. Looking at the weight belt and helmet, the massive air compressor and bulky canvas dress, the coils of line and air hose, Morey wondered what he had gotten himself into. Morey kept his mind away from fear of a "squeeze". Swallowing his anxiety, he dressed for the dive. The equipment was heavier than he had expected. The helmet, lead shoes and weight belt out-weighed Morey's 190-pound frame by ten pounds.

Fussing with the microphone inside the helmet, he asked Burford if the chin valve really worked. Burford soothed his fears. He put the helmet over Morey's head and screwed it down tightly, dropping the key in the slot and locking it. "It's sixty feet to the bottom. You're on your own." Burford walked him to the edge of the barge. Morey stole a nervous glance at Burford, who pointed down to the ocean. He hit the chin valve as he jumped in and descended through sixty feet of icy water. A rush of noise as the compressed air filled his helmet deafened Morey momentarily. The water changed from a light blue to dark gray as he descended further. "I'm on the bottom!" yelled Morey into the confining helmet. "That's fine," reassured Burford.

Time had no meaning to him. When the tender called down that it had been thirty minutes, Morey felt it had been closer to only ten. Getting used to the feel, or lack of feel in the water, puzzled Morey. "Maybe I'm not on the bottom. I seem to be standing on something." Morey wasn't thinking too decisively. "You won't believe this, but I landed on a Ford motor down here." "Oh, Walt, those Fords get around," Burford responded in a quiet voice. "I'm on the bottom of the sea!" Morey was so excited. "Not only am I breathing down here. I'm still alive!"[8]

He was ready to go to work inspecting salmon traps. Salmon traps are much like horse corrals; only they are set at sea. The area enclosed may be as large as an acre divided into smaller sections. Salmon swimming up the coastline get into the trap and the only exit is through a series of fake leads that finally dump the salmon into the "jigger." A jigger has only one opening that takes the salmon through a funnel and dumps him in with the other salmon in an area called the "spiller." From the spiller, the tender empties the fish by the thousands into the cannery boat. Millions of salmon can be trapped and killed this way in one season. The traps are made of chicken wire, hung from the top of the sea to the bed. Every part is enclosed except a two-foot wide gate where the fish enter.

Divers are hired to walk around the bottom of the traps and along the sides to make sure that all the wire is held fast and to look for damage. Divers also check for holdups, spots in the wire that have been caught on a nail or piling sliver and have torn a hole in the trap. Fish could escape through this hole unharmed. Not only salmon get caught in the traps; divers have rescued numerous unwanted creatures that have gotten trapped in the wire mesh by accident.

One day, Morey arrived at a trap location to find everyone looking disgruntled and glaring over the edge of the barge. One of the watchmen was on the outer trap walkway looking down along the mesh lines. As the divers approached the barge, they could feel the pitching of the trap logs. A great black head appeared out of the sea right next to the walkway. Then a huge column of water shot into the air as the whale's head again sank below the surface.

The whale kicked and flailed about in the water while the men discussed the best approach to setting him free. Killing the whale would only attract sharks, so it was decided that Morey would go down and cut him loose. He knew the danger of getting too close to the whale. Cutting him loose would be tricky, for as soon as the whale felt the wire slacken, he would immediately try to bolt out of the trap. It was possible that Morey could become entangled in the wire with the whale, or that the whale could take him down too deep if he wasn't careful. He also had to safeguard his air hose because the whale's wild movements could cut his lifeline, possibly even tearing the hose from his helmet.

Morey sat on the barge while a watchman, who acted as his tender, buckled him into his gear. The bright orange compressor set off a clatter and the needle rose up to a hundred pounds. Climbing down the ladder, he held fast to two pairs of wire cutters and looked back at the compressor. Two black hoses, one his air hose and the other a rubber-coated steel cable followed him off of the barge and into the sea.

A shallow rush of air sifted through the loudspeaker as the tension grew on board. In a squeaky voice, caused by the use of an air/helium mixture, which was safer than using only air, Morey let the tender know that he had neared the opposite side of the boat. Keeping the airline slack so it would hang well out of the way of the whale, the men above waited anxiously to hear again from the diver.

He hit his chin valve and descended closer to the wire cage, following the wire until he was beside the killer whale. He was close enough now to see the whale's beady eyes. He started to cut the wire about six feet away from the massive black body entangled in the mesh. As he finished the bottom cuts, the whale burst forward, throwing its tail sideways and setting off a whirlpool of water. Morey clutched the fastened wire and waited for the whale to calm down. Keeping one eye on the whale and one on the mesh, he carefully moved around the shape of this unfortunate animal. Following the wire under the white belly, he finished cutting around the whale. All this time, the tender worked the cables, tightening and slacking the airline and cable depending on Morey's location and the whale.

Sweating inside his canvas dress, wishing he could stop for a moment's break, Morey diligently kept cutting. He knew that the top cuts would be the most dangerous; if the whale felt the wire loosen around its body, it might try to surface. The light from the surface filtered across the water as Morey finished his last cut.

Walt Morey (center) with his crew, Ken Watts (left) and Vic Gordon

Photograph from Peggy Morey

Morey, preparing to dive outside the harbor of Cordova, Alaska

Photograph from Peggy Morey

Without warning, the whale bolted into the wire wall. The surge of water threw Morey away from the whale and ripped mesh scraped by his faceplate as the animal plunged through the trap and swam away. Morey was thrown against the piling. Getting his balance, he searched for the ladder and climbed shakily aboard. As Morey waited for the tender to remove his helmet, he caught a glimpse of the whale swimming out to sea. This was only the first of many animals Morey would have to cut from wire entrapments in Alaskan waters.

Later that week, Morey was salvaging an old wreck, a tangle of steel cable clamped itself onto his boot. As he tried to pull the cable apart, individual strands began bursting out of it, slicing his hands. Blood was seeping all over, but all Morey could think about was how his bloody hands were a signal for sharks. He had to free his boot and get out of the water immediately. So, grasping his equipment with his wounded hands, he let all of the air out of his suit and hoped his tender cold wrench him free from the trap. Morey pulled on his line, sending a signal to his tender, who began drawing him back to shore. Morey was able to wriggle free from his near death experience.

Once, while he was underwater walking along the wire in the heart of a trap, a large sea lion swam right up into Morey's faceplate. His nose touched the glass and he let out a snort, showing off his bad teeth. Morey looked right down his throat and tried to figure out how to get rid of this pesky companion. The creature swam a tight circle around Morey, bumping him in a playful gesture. With the animal behind him, he was afraid to move. His airline was only inches away from the sea lion's sharp teeth and any action on his part might be interpreted by the animal as a game. He stayed still while the creature curiously nosed his outfit. Swimming around a second time, the sea lion paused in front of Morey. Fearing that the animal would rush at him again, Morey pulled back the rubber cuff at the wrist of his suit and sent a stream of air bubbles straight into its face. The bubbles smacked him right on the nose, sending him a clear message that the diver was not in the mood to play. Relieved that the trick worked, Morey watched the sea lion swim off into the darkness.

Sometimes a trap did not produce fish and, upon investigation, Morey would find nothing wrong with it. He soon learned that fish pirates were responsible for this mystery. By sliding up to the traps, the pirates could quickly empty a spiller. The pirates could sell the fish to the same cannery that had hired out the fish traps. The pirates were never prosecuted because the canneries needed the fish so badly that they did not care how they got them.

In the spring of 1951, Burford and Morey worked only thirty traps in Prince William Sound. Some traps were as far away as a day's run. Dives were becoming scarce when finally their luck changed. That summer, both Burford and Morey turned to fish piracy (a business which was recognized in the Alaska Territory as legitimate). They met up with one of the best-known fish pirates in the region. The pirate was looking for extra men, so Morey and Burford took the job. Locking up their diving supplies, the men went off in a forty-eight-foot seiner. Morey noticed that the seiner was painted a dull gray so it would look like any other fishing boat. He also remarked to Burford that there were two hooks above the seine's nameplate where a board could be hung to hide her identity.

Traveling around the net watchmen's schedules, the divers returned to many of the traps, which they had earlier inspected. Sometimes, when the watchmen were on the traps, they would look the other way with an exchange of alcohol or money. What happened between the pirates and the canneries was their business. "We need the fish," said one superintendent to Morey. "Down at the home office, they don't care where they come from. It takes 200,000 cases to declare a profit. I'll buy from anyone, no matter who they've stolen from."[9]

Morey's months spent diving and pirating, along with the people he met in Prince William Sound, influenced not only his writing but also his whole life. He had experienced a lifetime of adventure, and the tales he heard at the bars and harbors provided him with ample material for his writing. That fall, he returned home to his filbert farm in Vancouver, Washington, and began to write stories about his Alaskan journeys. In the book, *North to Danger* he recalls Burford's story of convincing a dive master that Morey was a professional diver. In 1964, he moved with his wife to a 50-acre filbert farm in Wilsonville, Oregon, where he wrote until his death in 1992, at the age of 85.

Walt Morey's published books include:

> No Cheers, No Glory (1945)
> North to Danger (1954)
> Gentle Ben (1965)
> Kavik the Wolf Dog (1968)
> Angry Waters (1969)
> Gloomy Gus (1970)
> Runaway Stallion (1970)
> Deep Trouble (1971)
> Scrub Dog of Alaska (1971)
> The Bear of Friday Creek (1971)
> Canyon Winter (1972)
> Home is the North (1973)
> Operation Blue Bear (1975)
> Year of the Black Pony (1976)
> Run Far, Run Fast (1979)
> Sandy and the Rock Star (1979)
> Hero (1980)
> The Lemon Meringue Dog (1980)
> Death Walk (1991)

> Morey's writing awards:

Dutton Junior Animal Book Award for *Gentle Ben* and *Kavik the Wolf Dog*
Sequoia Book Award
Dorothy Canfield Fisher Award

Gentle Ben was the idea for the motion picture, "Gentle Giant," Paramount, 1967, and the CBS television series, "Gentle Ben," which ran from 1967-69. *Sandy and the Rock Star* inspired the movie, "Sultan and the Rock Star," and "The Courage of Kavik, the Wolf Dog," originated from Morey's book, *Kavik the Wolf Dog.* Both of these movies were broadcast on NBC in 1980. *Year of the Black Pony* was made into a film titled, "The Wild Pony." (Disney Studios owns the film rights to *Run Far, Run Fast.*) Walt Morey wrote for men's magazines, 1930-1950, including "Saga," "True," "Argosy," and others.

Harold Maiken at work in the Columbia River
Photograph from the Oregon Historical Society (#CN 012560)

DIVERS WHO MAINTAINED BRIDGES AND DAMS

These men were the cream of the crop diving specialists who accepted the risks associated with their incredible projects. The wind and rain on the surface and the dangerous soft silt on the bottom can make these innocent-looking jobs more lethal than any salvage work.

In 1937, Harold Maiken worked for the Portland Gas and Coke Company, but he was hungry for extra work. He pursued his passion for the sea by setting up his own underwater construction and salvage business. Because money was tight, Maiken borrowed all he could from one of the few banks that offered loans without collateral and bought a hardhat outfit. Since he had a talent for building and repair, he constructed his own shallow water diving helmet. He walked along the waterfront and talked with anyone who could teach him how to use a compressor and pump. Then, he returned home and built his own air compressor, a hand pump, and installed radio earphones. After all of his preparation, he was ready for the diving business.

On his first paid diving job, he was hired to recover a 32-horsepower outboard motor in the Portland Harbor. The water was fifty-feet deep, and he could only stay down for an hour at a time. By locating the boat on his first dive, he made $25 - equal to a week's wage at the gas company. Word got out that Maiken was an efficient diver. Small jobs came along and his reputation grew. He made more money on his weekend dives then at his regular job. Soon he was able to buy better gear and increase his dive time.

Maiken had joined the Marines in 1941 and served four years, and then he did another six years as a Marine reservist. There was a shortage of construction divers in the service, so he was held out of combat and stayed busy doing his work underwater, from Alaska all the way down to Mexico. During the war, he salvaged ships, inspected projects and helped build launch-ways for the U.S. Marines, all the while learning diving techniques from the other Marine divers.

When the war ended, Maiken created a back yard diving service, specializing in salvage and underwater inspection work. He got many young divers who wanted to work for him and get paid to learn the skills of commercial diving. Maiken kept expanding his diving service and salvage company.

In 1945, Maiken teamed up with Bob Patching, another skilled diver, and they merged their independent companies into one, calling it Commercial Divers, Inc. The new business was located on the shore of the Willamette River in Portland, Oregon. They had four regular divers and two apprentices on call. Commercial Divers soon became one of the top diving firms in the Northwest. Divers such as Jerry Hiersche and Jack Gallagher raised the standard of construction diving around the region. In 1946, Patching retired to his farm in southeastern Oregon. Maiken bought him out and kept the company active along the Columbia River building and repairing bridges and dams.

Maiken ran his business as sharply as his expectations for his divers. He considered any diver an apprentice until he had completed five years of commercial diving. He wanted them to be able to handle explosives underwater, cut steel with gas and electric torches, and do carpenter work and rigging. All of his men had to know how to examine a vessel's hull, perform all kinds of bridge and dam inspections, and have the ability to work efficiently on all salvage jobs.

He was also one hundred percent behind each of his employees, bartering for excellent wages and comforts. He laid out his contracts defining the pay rate by the depth of the dive. The basic rate of $100 a day quickly climbed, as the water got deeper. After fifty feet, the diver got an extra $1 a foot for depth pay. For any depth beyond 100 feet to 150, it went up to $1.50 a foot; from 150 feet to 200, his pay went up to $2 a foot. "After 200 feet," smirked Maiken, "as far as I am concerned, the wage goes up to $10 an inch." The pressure is tremendous at that depth, so a diver can stay down there for no more than a few minutes at a time.

Maiken kept busy, both diving and managing his business. In 1959, he had four divers on the Brownlee Dam, while he was shooting dynamite along the piers on the old Morrison Street Bridge in Portland, Oregon. Maiken had contracts with the North Fork Dam, the Pelton Dam, the Swift Creek Dam, the Merwin Dam and secured the underwater inspections for the new Interstate Bridge between Portland and Vancouver. That year, Maiken spent over 200 days underwater.

One of his most profitable jobs was at the Brownlee Dam on the Snake River, repairing the fishnet. The 2,800-foot steel fishnet was there to trap the salmon, but the installation was damaged. "The net was 130-foot deep and there were investigative dives of over 200 feet. That job alone came close to $300,000. We had divers there 10 months and there was all that depth money," said Maiken with a grin.

The following year, Maiken had his men clean out the underwater debris from the John Day Bridge. Also, they often did jobs for the U.S. Corps of Engineers, State Highway Department, utility companies building dams, and just about anyone else around the northwest who needed marine services.

Most of Maiken's jobs were both intriguing and hazardous at the same time. Maiken recalls one such job for the Portland General Electric Company:

"I was called upon to remove some stop logs from an intake to a draft tube from Lake Harriet on the Upper Clackamas River. A routine job, so I thought. The resident manager told me that I was to work on a pipeline that was not open or connected in any way. I opened the trash racks and went into the forebay. It was pitch dark. I had only gone a few feet when suction grabbed me and I was pulled into an opening leading into an adjoining draft tube. The opening was only about three-by-six feet. As I started through the tube, I spread my arms and legs to catch the sides of the doorway. I had on a lifeline and an extra strong air hose. I yelled over my phone to tell my tender, Joe Dittler, what was going on and to pull hard on everything.

Fortunately, we had an extra man on board. He held on to my lifeline. It took a lot of pulling by all three of us to break me loose from the deadly suction. If we hadn't accomplished this, I would have had a seven-mile trip to and through the turbines at Three Lynx Powerhouse. After it was all over and the offending draft tube was shut off, the project resident manager took another look at the blueprints and confirmed that the three-by-six-foot opening between the two forebays was not shown on the print - an omission that nearly cost me my life."[10]

Another time in 1946, when Maiken was hired to help build the dry docks on Swan Island in Portland, he was trapped in a cave-in while working. The divers there were pulling sheet piling about five feet below the Columbia River bottom. The bottom was sandy and one splice had broken; Maiken went down to retrieve it. In order to grasp it, he had to dig down in the sand using a high-pressure water jet with a special nozzle that pushed the water in both directions at 200 pounds of pressure. Maiken had cleared a hole about three feet wide down towards the splice and signaled for a glomer (a lifting clamp) when suddenly someone above turned off his water jet. The jet was keeping the hole open: when it was shut off, the hole quickly filled back up with sand. Maiken was buried on the river bottom with just his head and shoulders above the sand; he could not move.

Still clutching the jet nozzle in his hand, he was afraid to tell his young tender that he was buried for fear the boy might yank on his airline. Calmly, Maiken spoke into his telephone, "Hey, someone turned off the water and I'm not finished." After a few frightening minutes the water came back on, and the distressed diver was able to direct his cramped hand through the water and inched himself free. Each time he loosened his arm, the sand would settle back down on top of him. Finally, after an hour of exhausting struggle, he was free from the sand casket.

Maiken believed that the most dangerous conditions were found in the Columbia River and its tributaries. He knew the river was swift, and its deep, muddy waters forced divers to rely heavily on their sense of touch. Maiken respected any diver who braved the muddy Columbia. "A diver trained in the Columbia River area can work anywhere in the world," Maiken once said. "These men work by feel, just as a blind man does. It is surprising how soon one adapts. Many times I have gone on a job with a blank picture in my mind. Each thing I touched added to the picture; in time the picture would be full, and I could refer to it whenever I needed. I developed much respect and understanding for the blind people and how they are able to operate. I even learned to work an underwater gas-cutting torch by its sound. Believe it or not, when cutting steel, the torch gives off a completely different sound than when it is preheating."[11]

Because of Maiken's reputation, he was hired to be a water inspector for the U.S. Corps of Engineers. He was asked to inspect a cofferdam on the Columbia River in The Dalles, Oregon. (A cofferdam is a watertight cell that is formed by driving interlocking steel sheet pilings into the bottom. The water is pumped out to allow a dry space for construction or repair.) Maiken was asked to stop the potential flooding of the dam. He assigned three divers to clear all the loose material along the riverside next to the cofferdam cells and to seal those cells with grout bags composed of a sand and cement mixture. Maiken came by to survey the day's progress when a diver informed him that there was still a leak in the cells. A small seepage was pulling water into the cofferdam.

Maiken informed the men that he would go down and examine the trouble himself. He dressed and signaled a tender that he was going down. As Maiken descended to about thirty-five feet deep, the water began sucking him into the grating on the bottom of the cell. He could not move and was trapped on the grating. After several minutes, with the help of his men above, he pulled himself free. While he was heading towards the surface, the men onshore felt gravel fall out from under their feet. The vibration increased and the bank began falling into the water

As soon as Maiken made it safely out, the Resident Engineer, Colonel Elders, ordered all men to throw grout bags overboard against the cell wall. The water was to suck these bags into the leak and seal it. It took over a hundred bags of grout to stop the gravel from sliding down the outside of the cell. The men knew if they could not stop this leak, they could lose several cells and flood the construction area where men and equipment were located. When the situation was in hand, Maiken went down again to inspect the area. He ordered the men to drop off another fifty bags to reinforce the foundation of the cell, and then the crew finished repairing the cofferdam. His work was a success.

In 1952, the U.S. Corps of Engineers chose the Big Eddy, four miles east of The Dalles, Oregon, as a possible site for a new dam. The Dalles was named by French voyageurs in 1845 as "Les Dalles du Columbia" for its swift water flowing through a narrow basalt trough. This was to be a major link for the Columbia basin and would provide hydroelectric power for the region. Congress instructed the Army Corp of Engineers to prepare a review report for The Dalles Dam project. The engineers had to know the nature and conformation of the deep river bottom beneath the swirling waters of the eddy near the end of the Celilo Canal. Several diving firms were consulted, including some companies from California, but these companies said without hesitation that this job could not be done.

Knowing how determined Maiken had been on his past jobs, they hired him to explore three possible dam sites in the river that had to be surveyed and four dives were to be made at each site. Anticipating diving around 200 feet into the water, Maiken, with Joe D. Campbell of the Pacific Diving and Salvage Company, undertook this dangerous inspection. They hired Bob Patching, Ed Worack and Axel Olsen for this project.

The men loaded air compressors and rigging tools onto an army barge that was maneuvered into midstream of the Columbia. The barge was held in position by five lines anchored to the rocks on both sides of the river. A wooden diving stage was assembled to a downward line anchored to the river bottom. Without this specific layout, a diver and his gear could never have reached the floor of the river. Instead, he would have trailed downstream from the barge like a trolling line in the current.

When everything was ready, the divers climbed down from the rear of the barge and began their exceptionally risky and deep operational dives. The first man to go down was Patching. He had been a diver since 1918, and had worked on the Golden Gate and Tacoma-Narrows Bridges; he was one of the most experienced divers on the coast. Patching was a tall, full-bodied man, which was a disadvantage for a diver. It has been found that corpulent men are far more apt to get the bends than lean men since fatty tissue absorbs more of the dangerous nitrogen bubbles than either muscle or sinew. But the men knew Patching was good, despite his weight. Maiken had lured him out of his retirement just for this job.

Patching got into his diving dress, secured his lead-soled boots, and made sure his woolens were strapped in. (Boots then were made of lead and copper weighing twelve-and-a-half pounds each.) Ken Cook, his tender, screwed on Patching's fifty-four-pound helmet and clicked the safety key, laced up the back of his dress and secured the weight belt, adding another eighty-five pounds of weight. The heavy leather harness was placed over his shoulders. The leather had a strap that went under his crotch and around the back, buckled in front on purpose to keep the helmet from floating off of his head.

Patching climbed down the ladder from the barge and slipped into the water. He held there for a moment to make a final check of his outfit and air hose for leaks before going down. Patching then yelled, "Going down." The constant hiss of air coming and going through the tiny openings in the exhaust valve of his helmet pounded on his eardrums. His nose filled with the smell of metal polish and rubber. Twenty feet down, Patching stood on the diving stage and grabbed the descending line that guided him down through the menacing current. "On the Bottom," Patching reported as he landed on the murky floor. "On the bottom," repeated Cook. Patching grabbed the tag line in his hand, left the diving stage and began crawling upstream against the fast flowing river; it would have been impossible to walk upstream.

When Patching felt five knots on the tag line, he knew that he was only twenty-five feet away from the stage. The foundation of the river was bedrock, which had a light overlay of sand in some places. Patching signaled that he was coming up. The floor of the river was now ready for a more thorough survey.

"The water is both fast and deep," Patching informed the men. "It's the combination of swift current, the depth and the ice-cold water that makes this such a tough dive."[12] (Bob Patching made a record dive of 207 feet on that Easter Sunday downstream of the Celilo Canal by the southern rim of the Big Eddy.) Diver Ed

Worack of San Francisco said he thought the tide switched around on the bottom. "It confused my sense of direction on the dives," he told his tender. "Then I realized that the current was changing directions, first flowing downstream, then turning in the opposite direction and flowing upstream." The men continued searching along the bottom, and it took fourteen dives in four days to find a suitable construction surface. As they explored the bottom of the river, they created a map of the floor. "Just lay those cliffs on their sides," said diver Olson, waving his hands towards the steep, rocky walls edging the river, "and you'll have the river bottom full of stone. As for the old-time-pioneer stories about how the river current slackened in these deep ruts and formed pools of dead water on the bottom - they were right." [13]

When The Dalles Dam locations were inspected, the U. S. Army Engineers had a good map of the river bottom to know where to place the footings for the dam. After the survey was finished, Campbell told Maiken, "Now, I can tell you that was one of the toughest jobs we were ever on. You know, they said it couldn't be done!" Maiken sold his business in 1967 and stayed on as a consultant for another ten years.

The men getting Bob Patching ready to go down into the water.
Photograph by Larry Barber

In 1921, a young and restless fourteen-year-old boy caught a train from Chicago to go out west. J.D. Proctor arrived in Portland and took on any work that came his way. He was quick to learn and worked a variety of construction jobs for several years. While working on bridge ties in Oregon, he saw an advertisement about a new bridge being built way down south. Thinking they could use another hard worker, Proctor hitched his way down to California. Proctor was enthusiastic about the ocean world and quickly taught himself the basics of underwater work. He spent many days watching and questioning divers about their equipment and compression techniques. After a forty-minute conversation with a tender, he was hired out as a diver. Proctor's first job turned out to be a heart-stopping 110-foot jump into the San Francisco Bay on a cable salvage job. Once on the bottom, he had to crawl inch-by-inch, digging through the mud and dragging a smaller cable by which the large slings could be pulled into place. "I was so scared," Proctor told his friend Art McCray, "that I just haven't had any fear left in me since."

Proctor's big break into the construction diving world came with a job offer on the Golden Gate Bridge project in San Francisco. The bridge construction began in January of 1933 with the North Pier. The bridge was designed to hang from two 746-foot-high towers, and be suspended by two immense main cables that would contain 80,000 miles of wire and measure one yard in diameter each. Proctor was hired to work with Bob Patching and Chris Hansen to help with the building of the Golden Gate's South Pier and its protecting fender, with a trestle leading from the fort to the fender. Everything but the steel was carried across this trestle. The pier was to be made of 147,000 tons of concrete, extending 100 feet below the surface and 35 feet into the jagged, sloping bedrock. The fender was built to shelter the pier from stray, fog-bound ships. The fender would surround a football-field-sized area from which water would be pumped out. The concrete tower foundation would be laid inside. Once this was finished, water was to be pumped back into the 40-foot-thick concrete walls of the fender, in order to reinforce the fender against the current.

The conditions were harsh; the men worked in ninety feet of wind-whipped water. All work was completed in seven-miles an hour currents. As Proctor watched the divers enter the protective cage on the pier to descend into the water, he knew they would be shaken by the strong winds that had the power to lift the heavy iron cage and knock it into the water. He readied the tenders in case the divers came up dizzy from the winds. The depth in this job was especially dangerous and Proctor had to care for those men affected by nitrogen narcosis.

Also called inert gas narcosis, it is a reversible alteration in consciousness creating a condition similar to alcohol intoxication in divers at depths beyond 90 feet. The signals are difficult to recognize, its severity is unpredictable, and it can kill, from its own toxic effect or due to the resulting illogical behavior. The cure for nitrogen narcosis is a simple one, as the effects begin to disappear upon ascending to shallower waters.

Because of the combination of the high tides and the fast current in the straits, the divers could remain below for only twenty minutes at a time, in four shifts per day. Schedules were run so tightly that the men were brought to the surface without allowing for decompression time in the water, and they were sent directly to the compression chamber. Fear of the bends made the divers' moods even more intense.

The divers placed panels, beams, blasting tubes and 40-ton steel forms securely into position. The men on the surface shot timed black powder bombs into bedrock through the blasting tubes, trying to even out the rough terrain, often with such force that fish would be thrown out of the water and onto the south shore. Sometimes the divers had to work 90 feet below the surface to remove detonation debris. They smoothed the floor's surface using underwater hoses that put forth 500 pounds of hydraulic pressure. The divers worked blindly, forced to feel their way around in murky water and bulky diving suits. At the end of December, a diver who was trying to recover anchor pipe casings from the barge fell 225 feet off a steep bank of the east side of the San Francisco pier. Another diver attempted the same recovery but abandoned it when the sea began twisting him, between rolling boulders.

The Golden Gate Bridge project took Proctor two years to complete. After his success, Proctor began contracting divers for other pier and dock work, mostly with the Pacific Bridge Company. The Pacific Bridge Company was responsible for many noted achievements, including the Grand Coulee Dam. They knew they could count on Proctor for expert work and timely completion. Divers like Harry Reither, knew Proctor to be fair and hard working. Having gotten the bends himself, he was mindful of his divers' working conditions. He would go on dives first to make sure that the work was completed on time. One of Proctor's best working divers, Johnny Bacon, was on many jobs with him.

In 1938, Proctor was asked to repair the steel bucket at the Grand Coulee Dam. Although he was already involved in another construction job, the Pacific Bridge Company insisted that he go out to the dam site to get the job started. Proctor asked Bacon to complete the existing job while he took three months of his own time to set up the Coulee work.

The water at the Coulee Dam was cold: the men had to wear two-fingered mittens to be able to keep warm in the forty-foot water. The foreman at the dam told Proctor that the divers could only go down for half-hour shifts due to the water temperature. Proctor argued that at forty feet, his divers could stay down three and half hours at a time. They would go down once in the morning and once in the afternoon. At this depth, Proctor explained that they would have to decompress twice as long on the first dive, so they could go down again.

The foreman scoffed at him, so Proctor went into the water himself to prove it could be done. He got on his gear and smeared his hands with deep heating oil before putting on his canvas gloves. He wore two suits of woolen underwear beneath his diving dress. The foreman was stunned when Proctor came up after three-and-half-hours. When the tender removed Proctor's gloves, his hands were still warm! After that, the foremen never questioned any of Proctor's decisions.

In 1940, the Tacoma-Narrows Bridge, one of the longest single-span suspension bridges at the time, collapsed due to a 42-mile-per-hour wind storm. It had only been in use for four months. The tower apparently had been poorly set into position on the sloping side of the pier. A windstorm that hit the tower on Halloween set up harmonic swaying that finally tore loose the tower and the steel-form unit that was supporting it, sending everything crashing into the water. In December of that same year, another storm hit with equal ferocity.

Proctor was asked to help salvage the damaged bridge. He knew this would be a huge job, and it would take every diver available. He asked his colleague, Art McCray, to repair the damage to the site of the Tacoma-Narrows Bridge with him. Both men sent out divers to recover the lost tower and its lost forms after the storm. They rebuilt the shattered bridge by setting the towers back into position on the sloping south side of the pier, stiffening the struts, and adding open trusses in the roadway to let wind through. (In 1998, several Washington counties approved a ballot measure to create a second Narrows span. Construction of the new span, which will run next to the existing bridge, began on October 4, 2002, and is scheduled to be completed in 2007.)

A few years later, Proctor had one of his most hazardous jobs. He was sent to San Francisco Bay in July 1944. There he successfully salvaged two munitions ships that had exploded and sank at Port Chicago. Port Chicago was the only Pacific Coast port loading ammunition for the war in the Pacific. It was a dangerous job from the start. The divers had to go down in black water and had to pry open the freight cars and feel for the live ammo. Each one of the bombs was cradled in a solid wooden crate. To open this deadly cargo, Proctor had to use a handsaw, so as not to create much movement in the water. A munitions specialist from Washington D.C. panicked when Proctor brought the first bomb on board. The government was so impressed with his salvage work, the Navy awarded Proctor a special endowment. More than ever his name was synonymous with excellence, and he was in demand for other impossible dives.

Proctor was asked to assist in the repair of the new Kingsley Dam, eight miles northeast of Ogallala, Nebraska, then one of the largest earthen dams in the world. The Tri-County Project of the Central Nebraska Public Power and Irrigation District had built the dam to store water for power generation and irrigation and to aid in the control of floodwater. The dam stands over 162 feet and it stretches more than 3 miles across the North Platte River. It has gates along the bottom to control the normal release of water from the reservoir. Two structures were used to regulate the flow of river water from this huge reservoir. The outlet tower structure had four auxiliary portal gates (which did not usually operate) on the exterior of the tower on the bottom of the reservoir. The regular release of water was controlled by water coming through the portal openings, below the ring gate and down in a concrete pipe. This twenty-foot-wide pipe ran entirely through the base of the dam. For some unknown reason, the giant ring gate inside the bottom of the outlet tower failed. Two of the auxiliary portal gates on the outside were both jammed and would not close. This created a flood of water at sixty-pound pressure flowing through the gates.

Proctor was called in to supervise the job of installing a new ring gate. He hired three experienced divers for this 132-foot dive job. First, these divers had to stop the leaks in the gate working with the men on the barge. Proctor examined the damaged portal gates himself, done by feel alone in the pitch-black depth. Below, a tremendous suction caused by the water going through the portals near the gates made the divers leery of any sudden movements. One diver did get caught in the suction and was held fast to the portals. The others pulled him loose, jarring one glove off into the water. By remaining calm, he held his arm close to his side, keeping the air from rapidly escaping his suit. Overall, the men completed the dangerous job safely and on time.

Proctor spent his life constructing and repairing bridges, dams, and roadways, all of which are still in use today. He had acquired numerous skills that he used underwater while daring the murderous physical hardships of diving. He took on many duties that other outfits had turned down, knowing he had skillful divers at hand.

Jim Colby, Blackie Blackburn, Red Bingham, and Art McCray
Photograph from Red Bingham

A Look at Some Specific Dive Jobs:

THE DIAMOND KNOT DISASTER

The waters along the Strait of Juan de Fuca are incredibly unpredictable. In the early morning of August 13, 1947, the waters were especially rough and angry as the *MS Diamond Knot* passed near Ediz Hook, Port Angeles on her way to Seattle. A fog encased the harbor, blocking all visibility both along the shore and over the water. With her holds packed full of salmon from the Bristol Bay ports, Alaska, the 5,525-ton freighter owned by the U.S. Maritime Commission and under the command of the Alaska Steamship Company, was inbound and cutting through the thick fog blanket heading to Puget Sound.

She carried over 154,316 cases (over 7 million cans) of choice salmon: Red, Chum, King, and Coho. Her cargo was the property of the three largest food processors and packers in the world. In addition to the salmon, she carried 50,000 gallons of herring oil and an array of canning equipment, labels and 155 barrels of salt fish. Every possible inch, from holds to the deck, was packed with a cargo valued at more than $3,500,000.

Outbound from Seattle that same morning was the 10,681-ton freighter, the *Fenn Victory*. She was only carrying 200 tons of miscellaneous cargo in her holds, which made her bow ride high in the water. In the midst of the dense fog at 1:15 am, about three miles off Race Rocks, in the Strait of Juan de Fuca, the bow of the *Fenn Victory* slammed fourteen feet into the *Diamond Knot's* starboard side. The fierce collision of the *Fenn Victory* took the decks of the *Diamond Knot* down.

The U.S. Coast Guard received the ships' distress signals and quickly called for the Pacific Salvage Company out of Victoria, British Columbia, and the Foss Launch & Tug Co. from Port Angeles, Washington, to come to their aid. When the first signal "Mayday" rang over the radio, Captain Joe Tisdale answered the call. He was commanding the *Foss 21*, a tug built in 1900 in Tacoma. She had a 400-horsepower engine, was 80-feet long and carried the name, *"Fearless."*

At the news of the collision, the *Salvage King* was sent out from Canada to Washington; another tug, the *Matilda Foss* also crawled through the fog. All three vessels were traveling towards the damaged freighters. The distress signals of the *Fenn Victory* guided the *Foss 21* and the *Matilda Foss*. They were the first two tugs to arrive at the collision site. (Against the wishes of the Canadian government, the damaged ships became the responsibility of the United States, as they were the first tugs to arrive.)

The rescue teams saw that with her side ripped open, the water swallowed the *Fenn Victory's* main deck. Both ships were wrapped together and heading westward into the Straits. The crew of the *Fenn Victory* would not back away from the

Diamond Knot for fear that they, too, would sink. With two tugs there to assist them, the men quickly brought on board cutting torches and burning equipment to cut the ships apart. Once the forecastle of the *Fenn Victory* was free from the crosstrees on the mainmast of the *Diamond Knot*, she sailed into port under her own power.

Meanwhile, the *Diamond Knot's* crew had been removed for their own safety, since the ship was losing her buoyancy. The *Matilda Foss* and *Foss 21* threw towlines to the *Diamond Knot*, stern first, as she had water pouring into her Number Two and Three holds. They planned to pull her towards the South Beach and into shallower waters. The next four and a half hours of slow gain brought the *Diamond Knot* closer to the shore. The hope was that once they had her stationed inside the Crescent Bay on the Olympic Peninsula, they could keep her afloat long enough to salvage her costly cargo.

Water flowing off of Tongue Point Reef hitting the entrance of the Crescent Bay made it impossible to save the *Diamond Knot* from sinking. Harsh tides hit her side and water once again filled her holds. Captain Tisdale felt a strong pull on his towline and the *Foss 21* didn't even have time to cut its towline when *Diamond Knot* rolled over on her side and plummeted to the bottom, never to be seen above water again. Her decks were flooded and she was sinking under 135 feet of water. She was only a minute away from the shallows that would have floated her safely to shore. It was 8:55 in the morning and the weary crew could do nothing but watch while the sea claimed yet another victim.

The tug remained on standby until the next day. Finally, they cut their towline and headed back to Port Angeles for new orders. The sinking of the *Diamond Knot* was the largest loss of cargo to occur anywhere on the Pacific Coast. The Fireman's Fund Insurance Company and the Sea Insurance Company paid over $7,500,000 dollars for the loss of cargo and supplies. Salvage of the cargo was badly needed, as she held a bulk of the world's salmon supply in her submerged holds. The prime salvage contractor to supply tugs and equipment was the Foss Launch & Tug Co., from Port Angeles. (While her husband was away on a contracting job, Mrs. Foss started the company, Foss Launch & Tug in 1889.)

Walter L. Martignoni, of Pillsbury & Martignoni, was hired to oversee the salvage operation. Martignoni was one the world's top master salvors and had been in partnership with Captain Albert Pillsbury in San Francisco since 1919. An engineering wizard, Martignoni had earned his fame for saving several tugs, the *MT6* in particular, which sank in Hoquiam, Gray's Harbor. Martignoni not only rescued the 54-year old vessel but also sent down divers with heavy pumps to mend the cracked back of her iron hull and wooden deck. In 1930, when the oil tanker *Tamiahua* wrecked offshore at Pescadero Beach, off the California coast, Martignoni supervised another triumphant rescue.

In 1941, Martignoni restored one of the world's largest and newest gold dredgers stationed at Tuolumne River in California. The giant dredger, capable of removing more than 20,000 cubic yards of soil in one day, for no reason, rolled upside down and sank. With such skillfulness and dispatch, he rolled the giant barge, with its 250-foot arm, back into position, floated and restored her to working condition.

Only the best divers and crew were asked to join the fighting effort to save the ship's cargo. Art McCray of McCray Divers was hired as the dive master to salvage the *Diamond Knot*. McCray knew he would need exceptional support, so he called on Fred Devine from Portland to join him. These men ran the two largest diving operations in the Northwest. (It was rare for the men to work together, as over the years they had agreed upon separate territory. McCray worked above the Columbia River, Devine below.) McCray, then 35 years old, already had a reputation as a brilliant inventor and salvager. Among the eighteen divers hired for the job were Red Bingham, Blackie Blackburn, Chuck Smith, and Jack O'Brien. It was McCray and Red who reached the wreck of the *Diamond Knot* first.

Red Bingham had been working for the McCray family ever since he was a "grunt" for Art McCray's father, Walter McCray in the 1930s. In 1943, a surveying job on the Ross Dam project, on the Skagit River in Washington, was given to Captain Henry Finch, a diver from the oldest family of divers in Washington. As he was unable to complete the project, the young, eager, Art McCray took over, and Red began working for Art. It was on the Ross Dam that Red and McCray struck a lifelong working relationship.

Even though both McCray and Devine were well known for their inventive methods of rescuing lost cargo, it took the know-how of both McCray and Devine's men to figure out how to retrieve the seven million cans of salmon stored in the buried holds of the *Diamond Knot*. Their first enemy was time itself.

The divers were unable to survey the area until the fifteenth of August, two days after the sinking of the *Diamond Knot*. The waters were so unpredictable and the weather unstable, that when the McCray barge, *Diver III*, anchored over the wreck it was a bumpy ride for the divers all the way down to the bottom. The same force that sucked the *Diamond Knot* to the bottom grabbed at the divers as they tried to descend to the bow of the sunken vessel.

The survey showed that the *Diamond Knot* was on her starboard side, with her bow pointing towards Tongue Point and her rigging facing Crescent Bay in almost 135 feet of water. The *Ruth B*, a diesel tug stationed on *Diamond's* deck, was lost. Only a few barrels of salt fish remained scattered on her deck. Martignoni agreed with McCray and Devine that salvage of the *Diamond Knot* was unwarranted. The cost of salving the hull, assuming that it could be accomplished in time before the changing of the weather would make the vessel a total loss, together with the overhaul expenses, would leave very little or no value remaining in the ship. Also, the amount of time required raising the ship safely would exceed the period during which it could be assumed that the cargo would remain in salvageable condition.

It was clear to the men that the sunken ship would have to be cut up if the valuable cargo of food was to be recovered. Time was crucial and the men had only a few days to save the salmon before the sea would begin to corrode the one-pound cans.

The crewmembers generated ideas on how to proceed with salving the contents of the ship. It was first suggested to cut out the side of the ship and remove the cargo by using magnets. This idea was immediately abandoned because of its impracticability. The tins were too small for any magnet to penetrate under water beyond one layer of salmon. In addition, brutal tidal currents and the depth of water wouldn't allow the divers to be underwater for very long.

After many debates and ideas, Blackie Blackburn, a former gold miner and skilled diver from Rogue River, Oregon, sketched a suction system, which was quickly adopted by the men. The final plan, developed by the divers and salvage master, was engineered to force the tides to work in their favor. By designing two, twelve-inch suction pipelines, each with a direct nozzle at 300-pounds water pressure; the divers could maneuver these lines over the tins and suck them out of the holds at the bottom of the sea. Martignoni had used similar strategies before and was sure that this would work. The divers used their ingenuity and skills to develop a system that could raise a one-pound can of salmon through 135 feet of water.

The first task to be completed was the cutting away of over 90 percent of the *Diamond Knot's* port side to allow room for the siphon hoses to reach the tins of salmon. After the divers had completed the cutting, they set the hoses into the cutaway hull and began to remove the fish oil from her tanks. By examining her sister ship, the *Square Knot*, McCray and Devine were able to adapt the *Diver III* and a Foss Barge to hold all of the equipment and fittings needed to salvage the oil.

After the divers descended and secured a line to the *Diamond Knot,* they began plugging her sounding and vent pipes and attaching lines to the lower side of the hull. Along these lines, they secured fire hoses that ran all the way up to the barge. By creating 125 pounds of air pressure over the fish oil, they attempted to force it up and through the fire hoses.

The first time they tried this feat, it failed. The hose filled with seawater. Water, which is heavier than oil, sat in the bottom of the holding tanks. When the pressure built up in the holds, it was the water that was forced up the fire hose. Once the water was all out, the fish oil worked its way through the hose and drained into a steamed cleaned special container barge. The oil, worth over $22,000 was salvaged with very little loss.

While some divers worked to save the valuable fish oil, the rest of the crew worked with Martignoni on creating a suction device to vacuum out the cargo from the number four-reefer hatch. In addition to the *Diver III*, a flat wooden barge was added to haul and store all the supplies needed for the grand salvage. Knowing the problems involved in suitably anchoring the barge directly over the *Diamond Knot*, four large logging winches were first placed on the aft and forward ends of the barge.

These would be used to lower and secure an elaborate network of lines leading to giant anchors to be dropped in the sea. The divers were then able to lower and raise a complex array of lines leading to and from large anchors dropped in six different places around the barge. With the anchors secured against the power of the surging tide, the barge was rendered stable.

The suction device had to be able to withstand a colossal amount of air pressure being forced through it in deep water. Huge air compressors were loaded onto the barge in addition to massive naval fire-fighting pumps that would suck the cargo up from the vessel, through the yards of hose and into a container on the receiving barge. Two Caterpillar tractor cranes raised and lowered the enormous suction tubes and held them in place.

Decompression chambers, divers' suits, helmets, lead belts and shoes, miles of air and communication lines: men and supplies were coming from all over - from California to Canada. Many companies were building the needed devices as quickly as possible. Martignoni asked the Department of the Navy in Washington, D.C. for permission to use the latest wartime development in cutting rods. The men also received specially designed, extended pipe lengths for the siphon pipelines that were manufactured by the American Rubber Company. These pipelines were very flexible, with a twelve-inch discharge hose for the top end of the siphon lines. There was nothing McCray and his men could do but wait, it took time to have tackle sent to Crescent Bay. But time was wearing away the tin cans, corroding many of them and making the valuable salmon unusable for consumption.

Once all the tools were in place, the divers still had to get down to the wreckage and retrieve the cargo as quickly as possible. More equipment was being shipped and routed daily to the site. By the time the divers were ready to work the hose, twenty-seven pieces of gas-driven tackle and dive apparatus for the men and an additional compression chamber were all crowded on the barge.

In addition to the divers, Henry Foss, the salvage master for the tug crew, had gathered a host of engineers, riggers, crane operators, mechanics, pile bucks and heavy machine operators to an additional tug to be on hand at all hours during the operation. The Navy added a staffed barge to help feed and shelter the men working day and night alongside of the *Diamond Knot*.

Finally, on the evening of September 3, the *Diver III* and the Foss tugs and barges left from the Foss yards for Crescent Bay with all of the equipment that had been delivered, adapted and set in place. Because of bad weather, the barge was held up in Dungeness Bay for a night, and it arrived on the scene September 5 at dawn.

The first job was to safely anchor the Foss barges and the *Diver III* over the *Diamond Knot*. It took twelve anchors, ranging in size from 4,000 to 7,000 pounds, set like a giant spider web over the *Diamond Knot*. The gravelly floor of the bay made it difficult to secure the anchors. Eventually, they held fast to the ocean floor, attached by a series of chains. The men and the completed giant suction machine were an impressive site. A labyrinth of lines and pipe made up the suction device, which would be able to break up the rotten wooden boxes, suck up the tins, wash them through high-pressure water which flowed over the retainer barge, drop the tins and let the water rush back into the bay.

On September 7, the divers removed a plate from the port side of the *Diamond Knot;* they were finally ready to test the contraption that they had been engineering for over a month. Waiting below, Red and the other divers listened to the huge compressors and watched the siphon descend to within their reach. Instructions on where to place the massive siphon went from diver to tender to the crane operators via a two-way telephone system.

Martignoni ordered the air released from the steel manifold and the pipe gushed water from its end. The first task was to fill the receiving barge with water in order to protect the falling tins from the impact of hitting the barge holds. While the divers directed the flow, hundreds of cans of salmon began their water journey from the submerged ship up through numerous feet of pipe to the barge. The plan was working. Soon, divers were sent down to the number-three hold and the process began again. They cut a large hole in her side and a second pipe was sent down to remove the 1,599,696 cans of salmon.

Divers worked long and hard 120 feet down. They had to decompress for two hours each day in order to survive the long underwater shifts. Then the weather turned against them; winds snapped their lines and high tides bent the siphon and hindered their work underwater. As the storms reached severe levels, the divers were ordered back on the barge. No amount of salmon was worth risking the death of a diver.

The storms did not cease, forcing the divers to work from the barge and guide the siphon with rigging ropes. The crew attached lines to the exposed sides of the *Diamond Knot* and across her to each side of the stationary barges. This loop allowed the men to maneuver their barges' many anchors and direct the siphon into the desired hold.

When the weather broke, the divers returned to the *Diamond Knot* and fed the cargo into the suction end of the siphon. Each siphon could suck up about 1,000 gallons of water per minute, delivering about 800 cans of salmon to the top every sixty seconds. Occasionally, cardboard from the cases would get stuck in the hose. This was quickly resolved by shutting off the pressure long enough for the cases to fall out. The receiving barges were each filled to a capacity of 300,000 cans. This immense task took fifty-nine days of diving, with nineteen divers working around the clock. The last siphon was loaded on October 29, two and a half months after the *Diamond Knot* capsized.

By the end of the salvage, twenty receiving barges had towed cans of salmon away from the waters over the *Diamond Knot* to Seattle, Friday Harbor in the San Juan Islands, and Semiahmoo near Blaine, Washington. Under the guidance of John

Klaeboe, director of the Northwest Reconditioning Company, these canneries were well prepared to restore the reclaimed cans of salmon to a safe condition. Out of the original 7,407,168 cans of packed salmon, 5,774,496 cans were recovered. The 24,185 cases left from the *Diamond Knot* were strewn along the seafloor. To salvage another 10,000 cases stored in smaller holds throughout the ship was too costly. (In addition to the cans of salmon, two octopi, one five-foot shark, a diver's lead shoe and several shreds of the fish net were sucked into the siphons.) Out of the thousands of reclaimed tins, the canneries were able to open and safely repack 4,179,360 cans of salmon. Unfortunately, due to spoilage, over 33,000 cases of the recovered salmon were unfit for consumption and had to be destroyed.

Since it was 1947, the world was still recovering its losses from World War II, and there were still food shortages in many places. The recovered salmon was in much demand from Canada to Europe. The ingenuity of Martignoni, McCray, Devine, Red Bingham and Blackie Blackburn kept many people fed, and it kept the salmon packing industry alive for another year.

Over the years, the *Ruth B.*, a 45-foot diesel tug of the *Diamond Knot* was raised, repaired and put back to use. The shell of the *Diamond Knot* still lies on her starboard side in the waters of Puget Sound.

Fred Devine's crew search for the bodies of the two men lost in the locomotive that plunged into the Deschutes River near Maupin, Oregon.
Photograph from the Oregon Historical Society (#CN 007139)

WRECK OF THE LOST ENGINE

When he was asked to retrieve a lost train engine from the bottom of the deep, narrow gorge of the Deschutes River, Fred Devine had to go as far as The Dalles Dam to gather the right kind of diving equipment for this challenging job.

Shortly before midnight January 31, 1956, a 57-car Spokane, Portland & Seattle (SP&S) freight train on the 150-mile route from Bend, Oregon to Wishram, Washington, rounded a sharp curve two and a half miles south of Maupin, Oregon and splattered into a fresh rock-fall across the tracks. The rockslide had occurred in a curving deep embankment cut and derailed 17 cars. The diesel locomotive, and one refrigerator car unit loaded with canned goods plunged over the 25-foot embankment into 200 feet of roaring rapids in the Deschutes River. The engine car disappeared into the rapids, but the refrigerator car poked its tip out of the water. It could not have happened in a more dangerous spot than this wild-running white-water.

Ernest H. Barton, the engineer, and Earl F. Sutton, the fire tender, had been riding in the locomotive when it plunged into the river. The railway company was eager to recover the bodies of the crew and the diesel engine, which was worth $200,000. SP&S quickly set up a crew with railway derricks the next morning to clear the tracks and salvage their cargo, but these workers were unable to retrieve anyone or anything in the water. After ten days of hard labor along the fractured railroad lines, Devine was called upon for the recovery of the lost cars in the river.

"I don't see why we can't get this train up instead of twittering around the way these railway men want us to," Devine scowled. These sunken units in the treacherous waters posed a huge challenge that Devine had never encountered in his thirty years of diving. Devine took along his brother Morris, who had been diving with him for eleven years. Working with Morris was Lewis Smith, one of Devine's best men; he had been diving for him for 7 years.

Smith and Morris took one look at the river and decided that it would be impossible to search for the units underwater; the rapids would not allow it. The completion of this job would prove that salvage work above the surface could be just as critical as what was accomplished underwater.

Devine studied the river along the west bank where the rail line ran. It was impossible to work from there, as the front of the rail bed dropped sharply into the river. The walls, which hugged the river, were tall, steep and foreboding. He could hear the rush of the fierce rapids below him and could smell the fresh air of the Deschutes. Using a railway crane and boom was out of the question. The crane could never lift the engine free from the rock bed and a boom wasn't long enough to reach the center of the 200-foot wide rapids. "Well, we ought to have enough brains around here, ourselves, to invent something that will pull the 'ol girl up."

Devine decided to work from the east bank of the river, opposite the SP&S tracks, utilizing a graveled access road that had been abandoned by the Union Pacific

Railroad. It was lined with huge boulders, but it was his only hope to recover the engine. The narrow gravel road followed the right of way of the abandoned railroad, paralleling the crippled locomotive across the Deschutes. Since the water passage was bursting with surging rapids and it was too narrow for the divers, all they could do was use-sounding equipment to try and locate the engine.

After examining the situation, Devine decided it best to anchor a sea sled over the whereabouts of the engine. He had to retrieve the only sled available, which was at the Dalles Dam. He then sent Smith to Astoria to obtain several large cables and other tools from his tug, the *Salvage Chief.*

Morris and Smith helped set up operations with two Caterpillar tractors. By forming a loop with more than 4,000 feet of two-inch steel cable and extending it eight feet over the river with the 80-foot boom of a railway crane, they could drop the loop over the area where the 125-ton diesel locomotive was buried underwater. Using his famous block and tackle skills, Devine added several twists into the cable system, which doubled the pulling power of the tractors. Devine had used this method before when searching for distressed ships, but in the ocean, he had much better visibility. Several attempts were made with the steel loop, and finally, after many days, it appeared to be working, but there was still no clue as to where the diesel might be buried under the wicked water. A third try was made with the loop. The men felt it holding fast to something twenty-five feet below the river's surface.

When the location of the big engine was discovered, already having a dead weight of 125 tons and the water pressure of a twenty-five mile an hour current adding another 70 tons to its resistance, they realized that it was deeply embedded in the sand. To drag the engine from the bottom to shallow waters, Devine and Smith set up two Caterpillar tractors on the east bank. Each tractor could exert pull strength of 20 to 25 tons on its winch. Devine added two-inch wide cables, one of which was 840 feet long and another that was 640 feet, to a 600-ton rock high on the east bank. He then secured three bulky, 350-pound blocks into the rigging system. Even with this robust machinery, they still could not hoist it free.

By Tuesday afternoon, the tractors roared and strained, generating 100 tons of pull. The blocks inched forward fifty feet. Suddenly, the river slowed. The engine had formed a submarine dam. The water level near the boulders along the site dropped a foot and a half. The rigging on the cables joggled, and the big tractors roared again. Finally, breaking the surface, the bright yellow hull of the engine appeared. The tractors pulled on the lines and gradually the back end of the drowned locomotive, facing upstream, moved within ten feet of the rocky shore. Then, a loud snap was heard as the cable broke. The engine settled near the rocks some three feet beneath the boiling rapids. It sat right side up, with 30 feet of the 52-foot hull, including the cab, lodged against the huge boulders jutting up into midstream. A crowd of 100 spectators shouted and cheered for the men below. Morris sighed and patted Smith on the back. The applause was well deserved. Seventeen days had gone by since the train wreck.

With the engine peeking out above the waterline, the divers decided to risk going under. They took a small boat out along the cab where the waters were smooth enough for Smith to dive down and search for the missing bodies. Because of the pressure buildup inside of the engine, Smith could not prod the cab thoroughly with a pike pole. Neither could he get into the passageway alongside the Diesel engines on the left side of the locomotive. Smith found that both the two-foot-square windows on the engineer and tender's side of the cab had been broken out. The engineer's door was closed, but the tender's side was open. Smith found the body of Mr. Barton in the engine room and brought it to shore. Devine figured Mr. Sutton's body was thrown from the wreck when it struck a rockslide and plummeted into the river. (Mr. Sutton's body was found much later several miles downstream.)

Since the engine was still stuck after all of this effort, Devine decided on a new approach. He would build an A-frame with heavy timbers and try to apply a vertical lift on the engine and raise its back end from the rock ledge. If he were successful, the engine would fetch up on the east bank. He ordered twenty-four dynamite sticks to be set along the underwater ledge. The blasts caused the engine to tip wildly while an enormous geyser of water sprayed into the air. The men rushed towards the engine to wrap another cable around it. More dynamite and cable inched the engine closer to shore.

After nearly a month of a rescue effort, the engine was pulled to shore. Railroad workers took parts from the engine to the Portland yards. Devine had beaten the odds again with one of the most remarkable projects in his company's history.

Randy Greeninger, Russ Banna, and Pat Joseph are getting ready for a dive.
Photo by Rebecca Harrison

EXPLOSION!

It was December 17th, just a week before Christmas of 1976. The *Sansinena*, a Liberian oil tanker, with 60,000-ton deadweight, 810 feet long, 104-foot beam, 42-foot draft, and massive 460,000-barrel capacity, had stopped in San Pedro, California, to refuel when she exploded. The men could hear a low roar, not unlike an earthquake, which was quickly followed by a bright orange blaze, and an explosion that shattered all of the windows and sent a smoke cloud billowing into the sky. Eight men on board died and 22 were injured by the blast. Most of the colossal ship's hull had been hurled over a hundred feet onto the dock, while the broken bow and stern projected above the harbor's waters. The *Sansinena* would never float again. Two months later, divers from Advanced American Diving Service, located in Portland, Oregon, were called to salvage the wreck.

It was Friday, February 11th and Pat Joseph was tired and worn from fighting the water fifty feet down. For two and a half hours he had been cutting the *Sansinena* into sections manageable for a 250-ton crane to remove from the water. He waited for it to lift out each piece he secured.

Joseph had spent the last month working with thirteen of the Northwest's best salvage divers. Today was supposed to be his day off, but he had volunteered to go down to help get the job finished. The divers took turns going down fifty feet for a period of two and a half hours. Joseph worked with a strong team of experienced divers. Paul Greenke was working on one side of the ship, while on the barge, Dave Clark was keeping an eye on the gauges.

At 10:30 a.m., while leaning onto the disfigured port wing of the ship's bridge, Joseph took a deep breath before reaching into the bag that was attached to his belt. He felt for the remaining rod and was relieved that this would be his last cut. As the 300 amps of electricity and oxygen began to light, Joseph kept his eye on the tip of the white rod. He followed his hand through the dim water and reached towards the steel.

The touch of the arc to the ship set off an exploding frenzy that sent Joseph fifteen feet through the water. The shock, caused by the explosion of a deadly combination of gases within the hull of the ship, shook the pier. Joseph lay bleeding and unconscious on the bottom of the ocean.

The divers aboard the barge felt the quake and looking over the side, they saw an eruption of watermarking the spot. The tenders immediately tried to signal to Greenke and Joseph, but both lines were dead. Fearing the worst, the remaining divers prepared to go down. As soon as he felt the explosion, "Smiley" Vernon knew Joseph was in immediate danger, so he quickly geared up and began his descent for the rescue. Vernon followed Joseph's hose downward.

Greenke had been sixty feet away from where the explosion had occurred. He felt the water smash against him and he quickly moved from his side of the underwater vessel towards where Joseph had been. With only three feet of visibility, Greenke had to feel along the ship until he touched Joseph's cold and listless body, floating fifteen feet upward, tangled in the steel wreckage. Joseph's arms and legs were swaying in the water and his whole body was swaddled in cutting hose and line.

Joseph regained consciousness but was confused and unsure of what had occurred. He tried to adjust his air valve, but his arm would not move. He tried bringing his feet down, but they would not move either: he was frozen, floating in the water like a lost buoy. When he saw Greenke, he was barely able to tell him that he was badly hurt. He felt lethargic and fought to keep from passing out. Joseph felt warm blood filling his mouth. His eyes were blurry from the blow to his head.

Serving as a veteran diver since the World War II, Greenke knew how to handle dive emergencies. Greenke quickly and skillfully began unwrapping Joseph from the tangled rubber cable. He then reached for Joseph's harness and began pulling him towards the surface. Greenke knew he would get "the bends" by not decompressing as he hurried his injured friend to the safety of the barge.

They met Vernon halfway up, and together both men took Joseph to the barge. "Hang on, Pat. You're OK", kept ringing in Joseph's helmet. As they broke through the oily surface, an eager crew was ready to take care of the wounded diver. While Joseph worried about his numbness, the Coast Guard arrived on the scene, along with the sheriff, police, news media and the fire department. A medical team from the University of Southern California aided the divers in getting Joseph out of his dive suit.

In less than five minutes the men had stripped Joseph of his helmet, forty-pound weight belt, and had his rubber suit cut and peeled off his body. He was ready to be placed in the outer lock of the recompression chamber on the diving barge. Joseph was in great pain. He couldn't move his arms or legs, and except for his left hand, he hurt everywhere. As he looked down, he glimpsed the dangling, useless hand. He was terrified that he had lost the use of that hand and asked the crew if they would get a doctor to examine him. The pain in the rest of his body told him that he hadn't torn any nerves, but the lack of feeling in his hand frightened him. While they carried him to the chamber, divers poked and prodded Joseph, trying to see where he was most injured.

Randy James, another diver, went into the outer lock with Joseph to finish getting his oil-soaked clothes off and remained with him to watch for any signs of the bends. Once the outer lock was sealed, the divers were pressurized to sixty feet of water depth. While James removed Joseph's protective clothing, he checked for broken bones and bleeding. Just as James reassured his friend that he was all right, Joseph began spitting up blood. Terrified that this could be a sign of a ruptured lung or some other internal damage, James notified the medics right away. Joseph's injuries were complicated by the combination of decompression sickness and a concussion from the explosion, and so they could not remove him from the chamber. After another look at Joseph, James probed inside of the sick man's mouth and was relieved to find a chipped tooth and lacerated tongue: the bleeding was not internal. The blast must have slammed his face against the helmet causing the injury to the inside of his mouth.

With all of Joseph's combustible clothing removed, James carried him through the inner hatch to the bigger main room. While laying out a non-static blanket on the deck, James gently laid Joseph down comfortably on his back. Joseph would remain in the chamber for eighteen hours, with a doctor and his aide to examine and give him pain relief and comfort.

During these long hours, many people came to the site of the accident: several sheriffs and policemen, the Coast Guard and firemen. Eventually, an emergency helicopter was stationed over the barge, ready for the imminent flight to the hospital. The University of Southern California Medical Team supplied the critical assistance needed inside the chamber.

While Joseph was resting, the divers prepared another chamber to be attached to the end of the one in which Joseph was resting. Welders and divers attached this double-lock compression chamber by welding flanges onto the outer edge of each chamber, making bolt holes and fitting each with a wide rubber gasket. The transfer had to be quick and without any loss of oxygen. Although it was painful, Joseph allowed himself to be lifted and transferred into the clean chamber, where he would remain for the rest of the night. As the pain kept stabbing him everywhere, Joseph could only stay in one position for moments at a time. By dawn on Saturday, his oxygen-table had reached the appropriate level, and Joseph was moved from this chamber and taken to the USC Medical Center in an ambulance.

Joseph was placed in the neurological ward for an endless series of tests. He was finally given a strong painkiller, and some soup to sip. It had been over two days since Joseph had eaten anything, so this was the best broth he had ever tasted. In the late evening, Joseph was placed on a stretcher and loaded onto the sheriff's helicopter for a quick flight to Santa Catalina Island, where he was sent through a series of chamber runs at the fully equipped USC Marine site. They wanted to examine the swells Joseph had along his back and place him in a pressure chamber.

By Sunday, Joseph was able to walk a little bit by himself. But over the week, he didn't show any more improvement. The doctors were very puzzled but decided to send him home Friday morning. It had been one week since his accident. Joseph had lost over twenty pounds and still felt weak and unstable. Before his release Friday morning, Joseph went through one last series of x-rays. He was placed onto a revolving table where they could examine him at all angles. After a careful examination of each x-ray, the doctors discovered two fractures of his fifth cervical vertebrae. They were amazed that Joseph had managed to be so mobile all week long with a broken neck! Now the doctors secured him to the table and positioned him so he couldn't injure the now discovered broken neck. Joseph was put into a special Thomas neck brace and kept in the hospital five more days.

Joseph was able to walk from the hospital while wearing a rigid neck brace. After six months of healing, he was ready to return to diving. Joseph continued to work for several years with Advanced American Divers. He kept his work at a steady minimum while caring for his family and home. Now that he knew how fortunate he was surviving the explosion with a broken neck and the adventure of the work still excited him, he didn't take all of the dive jobs that were offered. Today Joseph is enjoying his retirement on a beautiful farm with his family near Hood River, Oregon.

EPILOGUE

Two exceptional divers from the Fred Devine Diving Company created Advanced American Diving Service, Inc., in 1983. Advanced American Construction is the now the parent company of Advanced American Diving Services, Inc. and the M. Cutter Company. These companies combine specialties to provide a broad range of expertise in marine construction, industrial repair, and diving services: heavy, civil construction in and around the water. AADS is located in Oregon City, Oregon.

Fred Devine Diving and Salvage Co. still operate on a 6-acre site with river frontage and dockage on the Swan Island Lagoon in Portland, Oregon. It has a warehouse and shop center including a 14,700 sq/ft is used to house diving and salvage equipment as well as mechanical, paint and fabrication shops. FDD&S offers a variety of underwater marine services, including video documentation, welding, cutting, hull cleaning, propeller polishing, environmental surveys, and general ship husbandry. FDD&S still owns the M/V *Salvage Chief.* Based in Astoria, Oregon, it is the only dedicated salvage ship still operating in the United States.

Commercial divers no longer learn to dive and practice salvaging with a garden hose for their airline and a bucket on their heads; several academies offer certificates and degree programs on marine technology. Such programs include commercial diving, dive medicine, and underwater nondestructive testing and wet welding. Both the Navy and Marines offer a slew of marine diving rescue and salvage programs.

Equipment used today in these diving companies is either pneumatically or hydraulically operated. Maintenance required on these tools are ongoing. Tools used in fresh water may need 60 percent more care than tools used on land. The maintenance of this apparatus increases by over 80 percent when they are used in salt water. One does not realize that diving can be one of the dirtiest jobs. Randy Greeninger, a diver from Astoria, Oregon, recalls a job in Anacortes, Washington, where he and other divers were hired to recover a large oil barge that sank in 130 feet of water. After every dive, Randy was "steam cleaned" to wash off all of the oil.

Even though technology has modernized many of the dangerous diving jobs, many divers still risk being killed every year. During the time of my research, four divers lost their lives. Most of today's work by marine diving companies in the Northwest is done by contract with large corporations and government agencies. The small, family-owned dive companies can no longer compete with these huge organizations. What keeps these men diving and working is that there are so few companies that survey, salvage and do construction work underwater, so these gifted men are always in demand.

BIBLIOGRAPHY:

Beach, Rex, *The Spoilers*, Harper & Brothers, New York, 1906.

Bennett, Ralph, Jr., "200 Feet Under Mighty Columbia's Waters,"
    The Sunday Oregonian, August 12, 1945, Magazine Section, p. 2.

Lucia, Ellis, *Tough Men, Tough Country*, Prentice-Hall, Inc.
    Englewood, Cliffs, New Jersey, 1963.

Martin, Robert C., *The Deep-Sea Diver*, Cornell Maritime Press, Inc.
    Cambridge, Maryland, 1978.

Newell, Gordon (ed.), *The H.W. McCurdy Marine History of the Pacific Northwest*,
    The Superior Pub. Co., Seattle, Washington, 1966.

The Oregonian: "Diver Buys LSM Craft," March 28, 1948, p. 29.
    Federman, Stan, "Commercial Diving Pays Well - But Danger Is Your
        Playmate," May 3, 1965, p. 30.
    "Fred Devine: Specialist in Saving Ships," January 23, 1955,
        Northwest Magazine, pp. 6-7.
    "Pacifica Parade," August 31, 1947, p. 3.
    Pratt, Gerry, "Making the Dollar: Diving Wage Scale High, Well Earned,"
        November 24, 1961, p. 24.
    "Unit to Help Rescue Work," March 2, 1952, p. 26.

Sloane, Howard N. & Lucille L., *Pictorial History of American Diving*,
    Crown Publishers, New York, 1970.

"Diving For Klondike Gold," *Seattle Sunday Times*, Washington, August 4, 1929.

"Experiences Recalled," *Seattle Magazine*, Washington, January 1964, pp. 17-21.

"Gambling Pays Off," *Seattle Post*, Washington, July 12, 1959, p. 29.

"He Dives for a Living," *Town Crier*, V. 29, no. 26, August 8, 1934, p. 8.

"Salvage Chief," Fred Devine Diving & Salvage, Inc., Portland, Oregon.

"Seeking For Treasure in Sunken Alaska Ship," *Plymouth Products*,
    No. 196. February 1930.

These societies and their data:

The Firemen's Fund Insurance Company
777 San Marin Dr.
Novato, CA 94998

The Historical Diving Society, North American Chapter
1223 Wilshire Blvd. #119
Santa Monica, CA 90403.

Seattle Historical Society
 2720 Lake Washington Blvd.
North Seattle 2, Washington.

Endnotes

1. Leone Baer Cass, "Girl of 18 Frolics On Bottom River," *The Sunday Oregonian*, June 15, 1913, Magazine Section, 8.

2. Ibid.

3. Kerry Walsh, "New Treaties Critical to the Salvage Industry," *Marine Digest And Transportation News*, November 1991, 30.

4. *Seattle Times*, January 1, 1939.

5. "Search For Body of Motorman In Wreck Started," *Oregon Daily Journal*, July 12, 1918.

6. Lucia Ellis, *Tough Men, Tough Country*, Prentice-Hall, Inc., Englewood Cliffs, N. J., 1963, 194.

7. Ibid, 204.

8 . Walt Morey, *4 Something About the Author Autobiography Series*, Gale Group, MI, 259.

9. Ibid, 260.

10 . Excerpt from Harold Maiken's personal diary.

11 . Ibid.

12. "Dive to Record Deaths Exploring Dam Site," *The Dalles Optimist*, April 6, 1945.

13. Ibid.

(Back Cover) Walt Morey, *4 Something About the Author Autobiography Series,* Gale Group, MI, 251.

Made in the USA
San Bernardino, CA
23 February 2019